BRIDE
OF AN ANZAC

My Life Story

QUEENIE SUNDERLAND

As written in her 100th year

BRIDE OF AN ANZAC

Published by
Gary Allen Pty Ltd
9 Cooper street
Smithfield NSW 2164

This (fourth) edition published 2000
First edition published privately 1996
Reprinted 2000

Printed by Australian Print Group
Cover design and format: Michelle Weiner/Media21

National Library of Australia
Cataloguing-in-Publication data:
Sunderland, Queenie, 1897
Bride of an Anzac, Life Story

ISBN 1875169814

Foreword

It is a rare and special privilege to foreword this account of "Queenie" Sunderland's life as it unfolds in this wonderful autobiography. Even more special is that it has been completed in this her 100th year, 1996.

"Queenie", or Nan as many of us know her, has been and continues to be an inspiration to all who know her, through her wisdom and her vast, near unshockable understanding of life's hidden rewards and regrets.

As you read and enjoy this celebration of a brave and true pioneer, you will realise her special qualities which have given her courage and strength to forebear the hardships and disappointments and to enjoy the good times of this 'ton' of years. For when we think of Queenie, we also think of her great wit and humour, her laughter (the chuckle we all love) and that envied encyclopaedic knowledge and love of learning.

To Queenie Sunderland, this book is her gift to us and the generations to follow. However, I believe her greatest gifts to us are those qualities in her which show us the strength to endure, the will to believe in ourselves and to have faith in God to watch over us.

For, at the age of One Hundred Years, Queenie our Nan, still spiritually inspires us and she will tell you her greatest strengths have always come from her unswerving service to and love of The Lord Jesus.

Andrew Robbins

BRIDE OF AN ANZAC

1897-1909

I was born on 2nd January 1897, at Beckenham - Kent. A suburb of London. My father was a foreman nursery gardener at the Crystal Palace Gardens, Sydenham. He was taken ill and died from gastric ulcers on March 7th, 1900 at the age of 32 years.

My mother's parents and her spinster sister Olive - that is Grandpa and Grandma Denham and Auntie Olive took all of us into their home called "Sunset View" in the little village of Easton, near Winchester in Hampshire. There was my mother, Ada Soffe age 28 years, my elder brother, Arthur Frank age 4 years, 9 months, myself age 3 years and 3 months and baby brother Frederick, 6 months.

We travelled by train to Itchen Abbas Station - about three miles from Easton, where Grandpa met us in his pony and trap. "Sunset View" was a large brick house built in the days when "The Family" occupied the front section and the servants the back section. There were two front doors, two back doors and two staircases to the upstairs bedrooms etc. Five bedrooms, so there was plenty of accommodation.

My mother stayed with us until little Fred was a toddler. To support herself, she returned to London and took a post as a nurse-housekeeper to an old gentleman in Dulwich Hill. It seemed quite natural to us that Auntie Olive and Grandma Denham should look after us.

Grandpa Denham in the pony trap

Sunset View my home in England,
Easton, West Winchester

On the lawn Sunset View *1904*
(L to R) Auntie Olive, Great Grandma Denham,
Great Grandpa Denham, Arthur, Cousin Gilbert Denham,
Queen, Grandma Soffe, Fred, Uncle Geoff.

We had little contact with my father's parents who lived in Winchester. They were much older and Grandpa Soffe was a chronic invalid.

When Arthur turned five, he had to go to school. The village school (now transformed into a private residence) was situated right opposite to our house, so he only had to cross the road. Arthur was my sole playmate and after a couple of days I was lost for company. As it happened I was crying pathetically when the local Baker called. He tried to pacify me but all I sobbed was "I want to go to school".

Charles - the baker picked me up, carried me over to the open casement window of the Infants department of the school - called to the Teacher (Miss Annie White) and told her the story. She held out her arms and took me through the window into the class room. She gave me a little wooden tray of fine white sand and a spatula to play in it. I remember it vividly.

Easton School, 1900
Window on left my first entry to school.

8

June 1900

Thus began my education. I attended school every day - nine am till 3pm without fail and at 3 and a half years old I was the youngest pupil.

Before I continue I must explain why I am called "Queenie" and not my given name of "Edith". My mother asked my father when I was a few weeks old to register my birth. She had chosen the names "Ethel Rose". To tease my mother in fun, he suggested an alternative "Edith Rose". (Rose was a family name for generations). Of course there was a reason. Apparently "Edith" had been a former girlfriend of his. Naturally my mother objected and emphatically declared, with a smile, "No Edith". Upon his return home, mother asked if he had remembered the registration. My father replied, "I did - Edith Rose". Instantly mother cried "Alf you didn't!!" He answered "Your last words as I left the house was that name and automatically I said it. I am so sorry. She will never be called Edith - she is my little Queen and Queen it shall always be".

From an early age Arthur and I attended the Methodist Chapel Sunday School and Services in the centre of the village. Grandpa Denham was a local Preacher, travelling in a wide circuit around the county, always driving his pony trap.

1910-1919

In 1910 at the age of 13, I won the Southern English
Counties Scholarship. This entitled me to attend the
Winchester and County School for Girls for three years.
The Grant which accompanied it covered tuition fees
only. I have always been grateful to my grandfather -
Daniel Denham for willingly meeting all subsequent
expenses including all text books, uniforms, etc. from
10/9/1910 - 1913.

Grandpa Denham was the Health Inspector for the
Winchester Rural Council - also the Rate Collector for the
district and a Director of the Winchester Jubilee Hospital.
In his prestigious official capacity, he was highly
respected.

During this year, my mother moved from London to
Salisbury in Wiltshire and opened a small business. This
provided a home for Arthur who had now left school.
Next door was a shop - "Parsons Leather Goods". Jack
Mason was the Manager. Arthur was apprenticed there
and so began a long friendship.

Jack Mason was a member of the Christadelphian Faith.
After many discussions over a period of time, concerning
Bible references and quotations, my mother was
convinced she had believed many things previously in
error. She accepted "The Truth" and joined the
Christadelphians.

Jack Mason (seated) 1914

One night in 1910 which was not particularly cold, Grandpa Denham woke the two of us, told us to put on our dressing gowns and slippers and accompany him to the meadow beyond the garden. On the way he explained the present re-appearance of "Halley's comet" had been predicted 75 years ago and was now clearly visible to the naked eye, exactly as foretold.

We saw a bright ball of light with a long luminous tail, which would not appear again until 1986, according to eminent astronomers. Later in 1911 Grandma passed away age 72 and Auntie Olive was left to carry on.

My mother had moved to Salisbury in Wiltshire because Jesse (one of her twin brothers) needed someone to care for his first wife who was seriously ill with Diabetes and unable to look after their small son and home. Mother stayed with them until it was no longer necessary and then decided on the business.

1913

At the end of my three years at the County School I realised I wanted to be a secretary instead of a school teacher. Not in Winchester but in Salisbury with my mother and Arthur.

Grandpa Denham was not very happy with my decision but eventually gave me two pounds and drove me to the railway Station in the pony trap. I settled down to my new way of life and obtained a job as a Junior Clerk in the office of George Hardy & Son - wholesale grocery, confectionery, tobacco and all soft drinks. They supplied all the shops in the villages and small towns in a very wide radius, extending into adjoining Counties. Delivery of goods was by horse drawn covered wagons.

There were eight other girls in the office. My wage was Two shillings and six pence per week but in addition, I learned typing, ledgers, journalism and costing.

Senior Staff instructed. This was the usual procedure as no Business Colleges were in existence. After I had been there one year my pay was increased to five shillings per week.

1914

War had been declared against Germany. It was known as World War 1, 1914-1918. Arthur enlisted in the 4th Queen's Regiment and was sent to India to train. The British troops stationed there were recalled to England for active service.

In the meantime I had decided to find other employment with better pay. I heard of a vacancy with Roper & Co, Military Tailors. I applied and was successful and received seven shillings and six pence per week. I was never happy there. All I seemed to do was answer the phone to Army Officers re-fitting or collecting uniforms.

My desk was facing a bay window which was completely blocked out (by law), against Air Raids. I had a single electric light bulb, with no shade, directly overhead. I used an all steel "Oliver" typewriter and the constant flicker on the steel keys in the poor light during the seven months I was employed there, damaged my eye sight. My optician prescribed glasses and advised me to change my job for one not using artificial light. I searched the local paper and found a Typist Clerk was required at Salisbury Railway Station, in the District Office of Spiers & Pond.

In 1861 the Melbourne catering firm, Spiers & Pond brought an English team of cricketers to Australia, paid all their expenses and guaranteed them 150 pounds per man. The sponsors paid all expenses from the takings of the Tour and made a profit of 11,000 pounds which they used to expand their business buying Railway Refreshment Rooms in southern England. Thus becoming caterers for the Refreshment Rooms of the London and South Western Railway.

I applied for an interview. The manager, Mr Taylor, gave me a thirty minute test - columns of figures to total and balance while he timed me with his pocket watch in his hand. That was necessary because all Spiers & Pond transactions depended on the Railway Time Table. (Head Office was in London). Three days later he notified me by letter that I had been accepted and I could begin work the following week (early in 1915).

The office was a large room with an open fireplace. On one side, the windows looked out on the "UP" London Platform and on the other side, the Devon and South Western Line. The windows were stained glass half way

up to afford privacy from the passengers outside.
It took a while to get used to the trains coming and going
all day and the bustle and activity they motivated.
Mr Fred Mould and Miss Winifred Tubbs were the other
occupants. Mr Mould - Assistant Manager and Miss Tubbs
- Private Secretary to Mr Taylor.

We had to use the subway to get to the "DOWN" London
Platform where the main Refreshment Bar and exclusive
Dining Room were situated. Above these two very large
areas were the living quarters of the sixteen attendants of
the Refreshment Bars (a Bar on each of the five
platforms). The bedrooms, two bathrooms, Mr Taylor's
private office, a staff sitting room, complete with a piano
and at the end of the long hall was a big kitchen in the
charge of a chef and three kitchenhands.

The girls who attended the Refreshment Bars were not
local. Most of them came from Hampshire. They were
quite well educated and proficient.
My wages were ten shillings per week, plus morning tea
and a hot lunch in the Dining Room every day.
It was a busy office. I had to check all the invoices and
accounts from fourteen railway Refreshment Bars which
comprised our district.

All supplies for each station was delivered to them by
early goods trains from London daily. Fresh bread, buns,
cakes and anything else in the edible line.
Hardware such as brushes, cleaning utensils, soap etc.,
were supplied as each manageress requested; also linen
and crockery and any other commodity required.

The invoices, requisitions, correspondence etc., were given by the manageress to the guard of a certain train at a certain time. On reaching Salisbury it would be placed in a Spiers & Pond box on the main platform. I cleared the box and dealt with the contents.

At this time, we had a family change. Our maid, Lily Emm, who helped my mother, left us to work in a munitions factory. The War was still in progress and not going too well for the Allies. Appeals were constantly made for every available citizen to help in various organisations. My mother (now 44 years of age) decided to sell the business and store the furniture. She volunteered for work and was given instant employment as Housekeeper at one of the huge Y.M.C.A. Centres at Larkhill Camp, Salisbury Plain.

These centres were numbered and called "Huts". There were five in all. They were very large timber buildings and catered for the Troops when they were off duty, providing tea and coffee, snacks, stationery etc. and conducted a good program of entertainment during the week, with Church Services on Sunday, led by Y.M.C.A. Officers. When I could manage a weekend off, I joined my mother at "Hut 2" and was given the job of serving in the Post Office section. An extra pair of hands was warmly welcomed. It was at this hut I met Frank Beaurepaire (the Founder of Olympic Tyre Co).

He was a Y.M.C.A. Officer stationed there after the arrival of the Australian Troops. In his early days he was a Champion Olympic swimmer. Many years later, he became the Mayor of Melbourne.

Before leaving Salisbury, my mother had arranged board and Lodging for me with a recently widowed friend of hers, Mrs Shergold. She also agreed to do my washing.

Queen Soffe

1916

All single men 18 years and over were conscripted for the Army - now more men had to be "called up". All married men 40 years and under had to report for Active Service. This meant Mr Mould had to leave Spiers & Pond, having passed his medical examination which Mr Taylor had failed.

My boss sent a request to Head Office that Miss Soffe be promoted to succeed Mr Mould. This was granted. I was now paid Two pounds per week. Owing to my new duties, my working hours became irregular and often quite late. Mr Taylor asked me to live in staff quarters with full board and lodging (at no cost) - I agreed. I had a nicely furnished bedroom. One of the housemaids made my bed and kept the room clean.

I still kept on our rooms with Mrs Shergold and I could meet my mother there when she came on leave.
On March 10th, 1916, I was baptised and became a member of the Christadelphian Faith.

Miss Tubbs (the Private Secretary), resigned to be married. We were great friends and I missed her terribly. Only Mr Taylor and I remained. New staff were difficult to obtain. All the girls were taking jobs vacated by the men. Eventually a very nice girl answered our advertisement. She was quick and intelligent and was immediately accepted. Her name was Triss Symons.

At this stage I would like to describe an incident which

was of great interest to me.

In 1915 Lord Kitchener (of Khartoum) recruited one
million men for the British Army. In 1916 he visited the
Troops on Salisbury Plain. The Station Master had been
notified of the time of his arrival because Kitchener had
to change trains at Salisbury Station for another train to
Bulford Camp on a different platform.

The Station Master's clerk hopped across the tracks to our
office and suggested Triss and I might like to see the
famous General. We went to the covered overhead
bridge and through the glass windows had an excellent
view of Kitchener's progress as he walked, surrounded by
officers, from the main platform to the short troop train to
the camp. The event had been kept very secret and there
was nothing to indicate something unusual was
happening. I have always remembered that tall, erect
military figure - every inch a soldier. He had a large
moustache and wore a long overcoat concealing his
splendid physique.

Later in the year he went on a mission to Russia in the
cruiser "Hampshire". The ship struck a mine and sank.
Kitchener's body was never recovered. (June 1916).
We had heard of the courage and endurance of the
Australian Imperial Forces at Gallipoli in April 1915.

Now the Australians were coming to England. Hordes of
workmen (carpenters etc. of non-military age or exempt
from conscription) were engaged to prepare
accommodation for them.

The tradesmen had a special train to take them to work at the various sites south-west of Salisbury as far as Warminster. On the Plain, Larkhill camp was also occupied by the Australians in 1916.

The A.I.F. arrived - Aussies everywhere. They had an office called the R.T.O. (Railway Transport Office) on the main "DOWN" platform, operating 24 hours a day and controlled by two Australian Servicemen in eight hour shifts. (Two at a time from a staff of eight). Seeing them daily when I cleared my box, right next door to them, we soon became very well acquainted.

Lottie Card, one of the girls I had worked with in Hardy's Office, had remained a firm friend. During one of my visits to her home, Lottie's sister Winnie came home accompanied by an Australian Officer, a Lieutenant Robinson.

Gallipoli 25th April, 1915
Anzac - Ted Sunderland

I left shortly after, went back to the office and thought no more about the brief encounter. Some three years later I met Lt. Robinson again, details of which I will describe anon.

1917

November that year was bitterly cold with strong icy winds. Early in the month on one occasion, Triss and I went through the subway to clear the "DOWN" box. The London Express had just pulled in so we had to wait in the Booking Hall for all the passengers to come through the ticket gates. It was freezing with the cold wind blowing in the wide entrance doors.

I noticed a big, tall Australian standing nearby. He too was evidently waiting to go on the platform. He looked so large in his military overcoat I said to Triss "Let's shelter behind that Aussie". This we did to our mutual benefit. As soon as it was cleared we moved on. The ticket collector, Mr Wally Coleman, called me over and said "I don't think you have met Gunner Sunderland yet, Ted, this is Miss Soffe" - introducing me to that "big Australian". (Triss had gone ahead to clear our box). I exchanged a few remarks with the two men - "Ted" went to the R.T.O. and I returned to the office totally unaware of the portent of that chance meeting, and introduction.

ANZAC - 162 Gunner E H Sunderland

Some months previously the American Army joined the Allies and prior to them the Canadian. They arrived in England first, were in Camp for a brief period and then dispatched to France.

During the past two years, Spiers and Pond were under Government contract to supply package meals to all the soldiers on troop trains on their way for active service in France via Salisbury to Southampton, then across the Channel.

Queenie Soffe, 1918

The meals consisted of two bread rolls sliced and filled with meat, a generous wedge of fruit cake and a fruit bun. Each soldier carried his own tin mug and mobile tea trolleys supplied hot tea. The platform would be crowded the full length of the train, with men and officers. "S & P" had a platform staff of girls on duty for each train. They had to serve the tea in very quick time because of the railway time table.

My job was to find the officer in charge of the train, get

him to sign the meal chit and write a short "yes" or "no" as to the satisfaction of the meal.

If a big reinforcement was being sent to the front, these troop trains continued at regular intervals all day and nearly all night. On many occasions I would still be on duty this way until 2 o'clock in the morning. It was a voluntary effort by all staff members and nobody even expected overtime pay. We were granted "off duty" time in return.

I enjoyed the variety of my work. If any of the managers in the circuit reported a problem and Mr Taylor was otherwise engaged (such as visiting Basingstoke on the Up- line) - then I would catch the next train to whichever refreshment bar required attention and straighten things out. A free railway pass perhaps to Bournemouth or Dorchester, or any other station included in our district, was a pleasant break.

Half way through November we actually had a quiet weekend. The weather was fine. Triss went to her home in Southampton. I was learning shorthand at the time and my tutor was a newspaper reporter who could only conduct his class on Saturday mornings.

Crossing the market place on my way back to the station I happened to meet Gunner Sunderland. He stopped in front of me and asked where Triss was (we went everywhere together). I told him and then he wanted to know if I was off duty too. Hearing the affirmative he promptly asked if I would accompany him to watch an

Australian Rules Football match being played in the local park that afternoon.

Having nothing else to do I accepted. My first introduction to Aussie Rules Football. I enjoyed it and have always been interested from 17th November, 1917 until the present time.
After our date it was "Ted" and Queen".
It was surprising the number of chance encounters we had with each other in the subway, during the course of our duties. Ted and I went for long walks, when we were both free, in the picturesque countryside around Salisbury.

More family changes that month. My younger brother Fred was eighteen on 26 November, 1917.
He received his army "call up" notice to report to Winchester Barracks for military service two weeks before his birthday, after which he was sent to Norwich to train.

We had also been saddened by the news that two of my uncles in the Soffe family had perished in the Siege of Kut, Mesopotamia.

My mother had not been well for some weeks following a bout of influenza and was unable to continue the arduous work at the Hut. She resigned and went to "Sunset View" to recuperate.

There was no movement of the troops over Christmas, so Mr Taylor gave us a week's leave. I joined the family and my mother. With our combined Food Ration Coupons we were able to enjoy a few extra provisions. The issue per person per week was:- one ounce butter, two ounces of margarine (which was often rancid), two ounces of jam, two ounces of sugar and eight ounces of meat. There was no choice when buying meat - the butcher just gave you what was available, either mutton or beef, whichever had been allocated to him.

I remember on one of my mother's weekend leave visits we submitted our meat coupons together hoping to get something special. All we received were some skinny meagre mutton chops. Liver, heart and tripe were all free of coupon. Bread was not rationed but by regulation it had to be 24 hours before it could be sold. As it contained a lot of potato flour, there were green patches of mould often found in it.

Food rationing did not apply to the Armed Forces or Organisations connected with them.
On Christmas morning I received a telephone call from Ted to greet me and let me know he had been transferred from Salisbury to a Camp at Sutton Veney - near Warminster. Back to 162 Gunner Edward Sunderland. 1st Battery 1st Brigade 1st A.I.F.

1918

Ted had frequent weekend leave. He came by train (about half an hour journey) and stayed with an elderly couple, Mr & Mrs Uphill, 30 Chipper Lane, Salisbury (later the birthplace of my daughter Daphne) with whom he had recently been billeted.

During January, I developed a severely ulcerated mouth and throat (I could only take liquid food) and my doctor certified me as being unfit for work for a period of three weeks. I wrote a brief letter to Ted (in camp), to inform him and phoned Auntie Olive asking her to meet me at Winchester station with the pony and trap, en-route to "Sunset View".

The next day she made an appointment for me to visit her doctor whom she thought he may be able to give me more relief. I won't go into details but the treatment Dr Wace gave me was drastic and extremely painful. It would never be given in this day and age by any medical practitioner. However, I must admit it was effectual and in two weeks I had recovered.

Ted wrote to say he had seven days leave and would like to come to Easton. He would stay at the village Inn and arrive at Winchester Station soon after 4.00pm the very next day. Unfortunately, the local Inn did not provide accommodation. I asked Grandpa Denham if he could stay at our house. Grandpa flatly refused. "An Australian indeed. He might be a married man".

My mother's youngest brother Geoff and sister-in-law Bertha, lived in the next house. We had a pathway across our gardens with a gate in Uncle Geoff's hedge. I went to their house and told Auntie Bertha my problem. She immediately said "He can stay here". How relieved I was. I shall never know what gave Grandpa Denham a change of heart but just before Ted's train was due at Winchester he phoned a Hire Service Garage and asked them to send a car to meet an Australian soldier off the Salisbury train and convey him to our house. The account to be sent to Daniel Denham.

There were no Australian Troops at Winchester so Ted was easily identified.
Auntie Bertha provided his bed and breakfast and the remainder of the day he spent with us.
Uncle Geoff was away in the Air Force but my cousin Reg was still at home.

Grandpa was quite sociable. He took Ted around the large garden (which a local gardener tended) and through the greenhouse (which was his own particular pride and joy), then into the meadow occupied by the pony. Just inside the gate, Grandpa had started to build a small shed.

To his delight, Ted offered to carry on with the work and managed to complete the job before his leave expired.
After that, as far as Grandpa was concerned, Ted could do no wrong.

On the last afternoon of our leave (February 23rd, 1918) Ted and I went for a stroll through the water meadow, not far from the house, where the River Itchen meandered. We sat for a while on a discarded post of wood by a little wooden bridge. It was there Ted asked me to marry him and I agreed.

I had never doubted Ted's integrity. He had freely told me about his home and family, living on a property near Dubbo in New South Wales.

So many girls during these war years had foolishly and indiscriminately married servicemen to their sorrow and regret. However, I did experience some qualms shortly after. I had been to Warminster to see Ted and as it so often happened, Australia entered into our conversation and it made me think of his family. I realised he had never shown me the first page of his Pay Book which specifically recorded Identification - next of kin - relation-ships etc. (I don't think this information was generally known or there would not have been so many disastrous marriages. It came to my knowledge through an acquaintance).

I reminded Ted of the omission and without any hesitation he produced the book from his tunic pocket and handed it to me. There was his number, rank, name and battery - all in order.

Second item:- Next of Kin: Mrs E Sunderland.
Third Item:- Relationship (blank space!)
It would have read either "Mother" or "Wife".

My dismay was very evident. Ted was no less confused. He admitted he had never checked any of the items and assured me he would have the correct entry of "Mother" inserted as soon as possible.

On his return to camp, Ted wrote immediately to his

brother and sister-in-law on the Farm and asked them to
correspond direct with me in reply. The mail took ten to
twelve weeks. Eventually the letter came and extended
me a warm welcome o the Sunderland family.
In May Ted had to report to his medical officer. He had
some very nasty carbuncles on his legs. The M.O. put
Ted into the camp hospital as there were indications there
were more to follow, which they did, on his neck and
through his hair.

When I went to visit him his head was completely
bandaged and each arm covered. It was a terrible ordeal.
Ted was an original "ANZAC" having survived Gallipoli in
April, 1915.

He came through the "Battle of the Somme" in France
1916 without mishap, but in early 1917, during a German
Offensive, he was badly gassed. He was taken to a Field
Hospital and kept there until he was well enough to be
transferred to a hospital in Bristol, England, where he was
a patient for some considerable time. His present state of
health was attributed to the poison gas still being active in
his system. He remained in the camp hospital until the
end of July before he was given the all clear.

We had not announced our engagement, having decided
to wait for the Australian mail with the evidence to satisfy
and dismiss any doubts among friends and relations. Ted's
long spell in hospital had delayed buying the ring and he
was now anxious to rectify that and reveal its significance.
As soon as he was entitled to weekend leave, he wrote
(no telephones available) and asked me to meet him at

"Slys" corner at 6pm the following Saturday. "Sly's" was a large jeweller's shop so I guessed the reason for the venue. I was punctual but no Ted in sight. I waited patiently. Seven o'clock came, still no Ted. Sly's put up their war time shutters over the windows and closed the shop. I had just decided to go home when in the distance I saw a big soldier on a very small bicycle - pedalling franticly down the busy street. Sure enough it was Ted and the bicycle was an old dilapidated ladies machine. He had been hindered leaving camp and by the time he had walked to Warminster the train had gone.

All the other decent bicycles in the very small town had been hired by other servicemen also on leave. Ted decided to chance it, paid twelve shillings and six pence for hire and was told he would also have to leave a deposit of one pound security. Ted rode the 20 miles to Salisbury in top gear and after such a colossal effort he still intended to buy that ring.

We went round to the side door of the residence behind the shop and rang the bell of the door. Mr Sly himself answered it. Ted explained just what had happened and said he did not want to postpone the purchase of our engagement ring until his next leave in case he was transferred in the meantime. Mr Sly was very sympathetic. He took us through to the shop and displayed the jewellery. The situation was ideal for us. It would not be called "romantic" but there were no customers, no sales pressure and the assurance we were not to hurry in making the selection. I wore the ring of Ted's choice as we left the premises with Mr Sly's congratulations.

September 1st that weekend, Ted became a Christadelphian and was cordially received by the members of the Salisbury Ecclesia.

One of my mother's twin brothers, Uncle Jesse, had recently purchased a bakery and cake shop. There was a large residence above the shop region which he offered my mother. Subsequently we left Mrs Shergold (now Sister Shergold) and moved into our new quarters. Ted and I had decided to be married on September 26th and thought it best to keep the tradition that a prospective bridegroom should not stay in the home of his bride overnight. Accordingly, Ted booked into the "Red Lion Hotel" almost opposite.

My brother Fred had managed to get leave from Norwich and was due to arrive around 6pm on the 25th. Ted joined us about that time and we had our evening meal. We sat and talked and waited for Fred - heedless of the clock until we suddenly realised it was 11pm. Hotels closed at 11pm. Ted left in tremendous haste. The "Red Lion Hotel" was a preserved Fourteenth Century Coaching House, built in 1320. The entrance to the wide courtyard from the street was made through two very large, solid wooden doors which were shut at closing time.

These doors had been securely locked before Ted reached them. There was no possible way of getting in and from our big bay window we watched his vain attempts to gain admittance. There was no alternative - Ted had to return to us for the night. (Still no Fred).

We decided to retire and went to bed leaving the bay window slightly raised.

The next morning mother heard voices from the spare room. She knocked and entered and there was my brother in bed with Ted!. No sound had been heard during the night. Apparently Fred had been obliged to change trains several times and wait for connections. Owing to a railway strike, the drivers were only taking the trains as far as their home depot.

When he finally arrived at our place in Milford Street, rather than disturb us and the vicinity by knocking loudly on the shop door, he decided to climb the drain pipe and scramble across to the sill of the open window. He made a good start up the pipe when he was unceremoniously hauled back down to the pavement, firmly held by a very suspicious policeman. Fred gave a convincing explanation and the constable slowly released him. He made it very clear he would stay and watch until Fred had negotiated the climb and entry through the window.

1918 - September 26

Ours was a typical "War Wedding". No motor cars permitted to be used for social events. No flowers were available and no icing on the wedding cake if you were fortunate enough to have one. For us there was no Church ceremony either. Christadelphian Ecclesias, at that time, were not authorised to conduct marriage services. Accordingly, we walked the three blocks to the Register Office, accompanied by Fred, Triss Symons and one of

Ted's Australian mates George Palmer and my mother. I wore a navy blue suit and white silk blouse, a navy hat trimmed and underlined with white silk and a short white feather boa.

Ted looked immaculate in his (privately tailored) whipcord khaki tunic and Bedford cord jodhpurs. His leggings and boots polished to a mirror shine. There was one great contrast between us.

Ted was 6ft 1 inch tall while I only reached 4ft 11 inches. There was a little bit of humour at the office before formalities began. The Registrar arranged us in front of a small desk, placing George next to me. George quietly changed places with Ted, explaining he was the Best Man. I think the Registrar concluded the shorter man would be the bridegroom.

After four years, the War still continued and food rationing was very tight. We thought we would have to forego a wedding breakfast and invitations to it, as so many others had to do. Our food coupons restricted entertaining.

To our delight Uncle Jesse and Auntie Annie offered to provide the breakfast as their wedding gift to us. Uncle had an extra quota for his business from the Government Food Control. I don't know how he managed it but he closed the shop for the day and gave us an excellent meal complete with a wedding cake which we and our twenty two guests thoroughly appreciated.

During the reception I received a note from Inspector Cooper, Salisbury Railway Station, to say the London and South Western Railway had joined the Midlands dispute and were out on strike. No trains would be departing in any direction.

I had told him previously of our plans. Four days later we were able to start our belated honeymoon.
First to Southampton then across the Solent to Cowes on the Isle of Wight.

Wedding, Ted & Queen
26th September 1918

On Monday October 9th, Ted was due back in camp.
He knew he was listed in the next contingent of
reinforcements for France, due to leave England two days
later. He promised to send me a telegram reporting
movements of departure. It duly arrived on Wednesday.
I asked my mother to open it for me. I felt it was
"Goodbye" and I didn't want to see it in writing. Mother
replied "You are a soldier's wife now - you must open it
yourself". With trembling hands I did so and I could
scarcely believe my eyes as I read the message "Expect
me Friday. Three months 1914-18 service leaveî. I cannot
describe my relief and thanksgiving at such miraculous
good news.

I resigned from Spiers & Pond. During the last week of
my employment I received a letter from Head Office in
London asking if I would continue to work on a part-time
basis for the same rate of pay. Mr Taylor expressed his
regret when I declined the proposal and with felicitations
handed me a five pound note from the firm.

Ted had been given the choice of six months home in
Australia or three months in England for his long service
leave. He chose the latter to be with me. I had no
desire to occupy myself with work.

Our time together was too precarious. We could not
conjecture in advance what might occur ahead of us, but
as it happened Ted never returned to camp again.
The Armistice was signed on 11th November, 1918.
The jubilation was overwhelming. The church bells rang
joyously - bonfires and fireworks everywhere. People

surged into the streets from every quarter. Business men closed the shops and offices and joined the crowds. Troops from nearby camps marched into the city, led by military brass bands playing lively tunes.

Later in the month, Ted became a victim of the dreaded Pneumonic Influenza epidemic sweeping across England and Europe. It caused hundreds of deaths - there were no antibiotics to check the onslaught. Fortunately, Ted made a fairly quick recovery but unfortunately I went down with it and was very ill for a couple of weeks. After our marriage, Ted and I had some serious talks concerning our future.

Was it to be together in England or Australia? If it was England, Ted would have to seek some form of employment. After serving in the army for such long war years, he was unskilled in any trade. He knew all about farming and farm maintenance as conducted in Australia, but to be just a farm-hand in England was very different and not very lucrative.

The other alternative to return to Australia ensured a good living on "Pine Farm", Ted's native soil and natural environment. He would also be reunited with his mother and the Sunderland family again.

To consider Australia for my own personal life and destination made me realise to accompany Ted overseas would be a complete severance from my mother, family and friends. I would be a stranger living in unimaginable contrast from city life to the Australian bush, leaving everyone and everything behind, going thousands of miles away, knowing only one person - my husband. Ted was quite willing to stay in England if it would make me unhappy to leave it. He left the choice entirely to me. The big decision was made very clear to me. A letter arrived from my brother Arthur, still in Mesopotamia, to say his Army Unit was being drafted back home in a few weeks time. My mother's joy at the thought of his return was a revelation. I thought Ted's mother would feel exactly the same way to receive news of his close return home. I too was now a Sunderland and my future - our future, was in Australia, without doubt.

In December Ted received "Notice" to "Stand By" for embarkation back to Australia. A similar notice came separately for me. This indicated we would not be travelling together in the same ship. Ted, being an Anzac, knew he was allowed this concession and if necessary would claim it. We set off immediately to Australia House London, headquarters of the A.I.F. to investigate. On arrival we stated the details of our business. We were sent from one department to another without any satisfaction.

Finally Ted requested to be paraded before a senior officer. This was granted and we were directed to yet another records office and there it was confirmed. Ted was listed to sail in "S. S. Oronsay" and I was booked in "S. S. Osterley". The officer ordered Ted's name and embarkation be transferred to "S. S. Osterley". My undaunted husband had won his claim.

Mother, Ted and I spent a very quiet Christmas. My

brother Fred's Battalion, the 51st Devonshire, had been sent to join the "Army of the Rhine", following the defeated German Forces across France back into Germany. Arthur was in hospital at Darjeeling, India recuperating from effects of active service in Mesopotamia with the 4th Queen's Regiment. Two of my father's younger brothers, Uncle Ernie and Uncle Bert had perished in the "Siege of Kut". The siege had lasted five months and eventually General Townshend was forced to capitulate to the Turks - the British losses were so great.

1919

Our departure notice came four days later. We were instructed to forward our luggage to the docks at Liverpool immediately and we were to board the special "Boat Train", Euston Station, London at 8am on the morning of January 10th, 1919, en-route to Liverpool docks.

We had a great send-off from Salisbury Station the previous day, although I had no relatives present. All the family "goodbyes" had been said at home at "Sunset View". Knowing so many people employed by the Railway and Spiers & Pond, we were not unduly surprised at the large number of staff members who came to the platform to say farewell and express their good wishes for our voyage and future.

We spent the night in London and next morning left in good time for Euston Station and the boat train. It was a long slow journey to the north-west sea-port and no provision of refreshments.

When we reached the docks, we passed through
turnstiles in alphabetical order and were given our
embarkation papers, cabin number and location etc.
The S. S. Osterley was a small 12,129 tons ship, still
heavily camouflaged from active war service. Only 150
men and officers on board but there were 300 Brides and
200 babies.

We sailed at 5.30pm sharp. A military band on the wharf
farewelled us to the tune of "Auld Lang Syne". I had
been cheerful all day until the emotion caused by the
music blurred my eyes as I watched the harbour lights
and England fade into darkness.

Although Ted was on the same ship, he was still in the
A.I.F. His long service leave had expired the day before
we left. All the service men were quartered on a lower
deck "Out of Bounds" to all passengers. They slept in
hammocks.

Prior to sailing we had located my cabin. It was a two-
berth cabin, one flight down on B Deck (I had not
relished the possibility of being allocated to an eight-berth
cabin down below, perhaps on 'E' Deck with so many to
share it).. Now however, conditions could not have been
better.

My cabin mate Dot Sutherland and her husband Reg were
waiting to meet me. A congenial couple. Dot was a
cripple having one leg shorter than the other and she did-

n't look very robust. Automatically I took the top bunk and soon got used to climbing up.

Parades over, the men were allowed to spend their time and their meals with us. The Irish Sea was fairly smooth and I was not sea-sick (nor Dot). All went reasonably well until we reached the Bay of Biscay, where we ran into a violent storm. Mountainous waves surrounded us and then plunged us rapidly down into frightening deep troughs. Heavy rain and gale force winds caused the ship to list. We were battened down until the morning when we were informed the propeller shaft had been severely damaged during the storm and we were on our way for repairs at Falmouth Harbour on the coast of Cornwall. Back to England.

Like scores of other passengers, I vowed nothing would induce me to rejoin the "Osterley" if permission was granted to go ashore. This was not to be. We anchored well off-shore for three days with the tantalising view of Falmouth in the background.

The delay gave everyone a chance to recover from the recent terrifying experience and settle down to continue the voyage.

The weather cleared and became warmer making travelling very pleasant. The coasts of Portugal and then Spain were frequently visible until we reached the Strait of Gibraltar to Gibralta itself. The Rock was an impressive sight, 1467 ft high. We were berthed alongside the wharf. As soon as the gang planks were in

Orient Line, S.S. Osterley

position, those who wished could go ashore.

In 1919 the town was not very large. Ted and I enjoyed exploring the narrow hilly streets and souvenir shops. We went on a trolley bus to the base of the Rock, then walked along beside the heavy mesh wire fence which protected it, hoping to see one or more of the famous Barbary Apes. A local resident informed us the Apes had retreated behind it after the British Army had concealed more guns in every accessible site across the gigantic landmark. We spent several hours there before departure to Toulon in the south of France. No shore leave at this port. The Mediterranean Sea was smooth and the temperature rose; winter clothes were exchanged for summer wear.

Dot Sutherland and I were quite affable. She was a very reserved girl and we had little in common except cabin accommodation. She spent her days in a deck chair up on the boat Deck. Reg often sat with her in the crowded area but he liked to play cards with his mates.

I had become friendly with a nice girl, Margaret Thomas was her name. She was well educated. She was travelling alone as her husband had been returned to Australia in a troop ship ahead of us. He would be at Sydney to meet her. I was often glad of her company. Ted had been detailed for duty in the Quarter Master's Store, which operated for a short spell in the afternoon of specified days. This was an advantage to us because the Quarter Master always gave Ted a bonus at closing time, such as a tin of pineapple rings or a packet of sweet biscuits, items we had not seen throughout the war years. Before we passed through the Strait between the Islands of Corsica and Sardinia, Dot told us she was under medical supervision and the medical officer had obtained permission for her to sleep on deck at night, which she wished to do. (Other passengers with health problems had been granted the same concession).

Dot suggested Ted might like to use her bunk in the cabin as she would not require it for the rest of the voyage. She always retired early which left the compartment clear for us. Ted accepted the offer with alacrity. A bunk, narrow though it might be, was far more acceptable than an army issue hammock. No objections were raised from any quarter and if a report had been submitted, it was never investigated. We had never imagined we could be so fortunate - a two-berth cabin to ourselves on a troop ship! We must have been the only ones on board with such an advantage.

The days passed pleasantly for me. It was obvious however, that many persons regarded the "Osterley" as being the means of transportation from England to Australia and nothing more. They could have been apprehensive about the future.

The women, (all around 20-40 age group) came from various walks of life. A very mixed assembly and the babies demanded continuous attention at all times. We proceeded to Naples, with its beautiful bay and berthed. Ted and I went ashore and walked through the ancient narrow streets to the city. Had a good look at many famous buildings, shops etc until the evening, conscious all the time of Mt Vesuvius smoking vigorously in the background. Ted took me to dinner in a very well appointed Hotel, where we enjoyed a splendid meal and excellent coffee.

Early next morning, we sailed down the coast of Italy, the island Stromboli with its smoking volcano clearly visible. On through the Strait of Messina, between Italy and Sicily, to Egypt. Port Said was a very busy place with trade as well as being a coaling station for ships. It is situated at the north entrance to the Suez Canal.

In an amazingly short time, we were surrounded by bum-boats. The "Osterley" anchored a considerable distance from the wharf. The open rowing boats were loaded with goods of all description. Fruit, jewellery, hand-crafted leather ware and souvenirs galore were manipulated by Arabs eager to sell their stock.

They hurled soft cane baskets with long ropes attached up to the passengers packed along the rail. The noise was deafening as each vendor shouted above the other in pidgin English in his endeavour to make a sale, with the passengers calling back as they tried to identify what they wanted to buy at a reduced price. Ted caught a basket. We had selected an ivory brooch for me and a leather purse for himself. His own knowledge of the Arabic language which he had learned during his service in Mena Camp (near the Egyptian Pyramids) from October 1914 to February 1915, proved to be very useful. There was only a brief haggle in Arabic and the money he offered was accepted. Down went the basket, back it came with our souvenirs and then it was dropped to the waiting salesman. The whole transaction had been very amusing. I had no idea what the verbal exchange accomplished but it had worked. The Arab understood!! I still have the ivory brooch in my possession.

Port Officials came on board and rapidly dispersed the trading boats. The coal lighters had arrived to re-fuel the ship. The carriers were all Arabs and with a jog-trot and a monotonous sing-song chant, they trotted up and down the gang-planks, in bare feet all day with their bags of coal. Everyone retreated to the starboard side. Coal dust had spread along the deck from the loading area to where we watched the activity. The weather was extremely hot and steamy, with no breeze from the water - an unpleasant acrid odour pervaded everywhere. Coaling completed, the deck hands soon restored cleanliness and we were glad to be on our way. We had a good view of the towering statue of De Lesseps at the entrance to the Suez Canal. He was the French diplomat who engineered the construction of the waterway in 1859. From Port Said, on the Mediterranean to Suez at the head of the Red Sea is 101 miles long, separating Africa from Asia. It linked up several lakes. We passed between sandy tracts of land - the banks of the canal almost level in many places.

Occasionally we saw wandering bedouins with their camels, the odd remote native settlements which were few and far between and very little vegetation. We had to wait a short time in the Great Bitter Lake for another vessel to pass and go through. The heat was intense and it took seventeen hours to reach Suez. The Suez Canal Company Building was a magnificent white structure situated alongside the quay.

There were no shore permits and immediately the formalities had been completed, we moved out. Before we retired that night, a general announcement was made by a ship's officer that the "Southern Cross" would be visible at 4am the next morning. This information was received with a rousing cheer from the Army personnel. I was curious to discover what the Southern Cross could be to produce such instantaneous enthusiasm. After Ted's explanation I realised it was a symbol of "HOME" to the men who had been absent so long - five years.

There was not many of them missing when Ted and I reached the promenade deck in the ensuing early hours.

Noticeably only a few women. It was delightfully cool, almost cold - a contrast to the daytime temperature. The heavens were sparkling and the group of stars we looked for was easily located and recognised with great excitement.

We proceeded through the Red Sea, a constant reminder to us of Moses and the Children of Israel who had providentially passed over so many centuries ago.

Before Aden came into sight, I had a bad bout of tropical dysentery and had to call the medical officer to the cabin. He prescribed some tablets to be followed a short time later by a pint of some obnoxious liquid in which floated finely chopped herbs of every kind. So thick was this mixture it was difficult to swallow without having to chew to get it down. The whole concoction was repulsive and to make matters worse, the doctor held the large beaker himself, relentless till the last drop had gone, my shudders of distaste completely ignored.

We did not stop at Aden but continued into the Indian Ocean. By the time we crossed the Equator I had recovered and participated in deck games, quoits etc., which had been organised for our entertainment until we arrived at Colombo, capital city and chief port of Ceylon (re-named Sri Lanka later). We were allowed ashore. We had to descend a swaying stairway down the side of the ship and jump aboard a small ferry to take us to the wharf.

With the rest of the ferry passengers we wandered in and

out of the shops. I bought a pair of little ebony elephants (one of them vanished over the years but the other one is still on display in my china cabinet). There were many fine buildings which attracted our attention. The natives near the wharf were annoying. They were so persistent in trying to entice us to buy their beads and postcards, we couldn't get rid of them.

We sailed the next day. A long distance to travel from Colombo to Fremantle W.A., surrounded entirely by water with no landmarks anywhere until the Cocos Island were sighted in the vast ocean. We filled the days with the usual shipboard activities and at night a dance or Whist Drive.

Fremantle at last! Passengers booked to disembark in Western Australia were quickly checked by the landing and customs officials. They left the ship first with the remainder on board waiting until permission was given to go ashore. Ted and I did not stay in the port but instead took a little short train to Perth. We travelled at a snail's pace with many halts along the say. The seats were not upholstered and I was greatly relieved when the ten mile connection with the capital was ended.

We made a brief tour of the city It was a change to see some modern buildings and a pleasure to shop without trying to interpret a foreign language. Ted took me for a drive through a section of beautiful Kings' Park with the Swan River and black swans.

We had afternoon tea in a cool tea-room and ate

enormous cream puffs - fresh dairy cream. I had never seen or tasted anything so delicious in all my existence. Adelaide was the next port of call, with the same routine. It was lunch time when we got there after a short transportation from Outer Harbour. With some friends from the ship, we went into a seafood restaurant and thoroughly enjoyed Murray Cod with delectable sauce and salad. After the dry tasteless fish of the recent war years, it was luxury indeed. We were all impressed by the wide streets, the location of the Parks and the magnificent Cathedral.

Crossing the Great Australian Bight, the weather and the ocean had been perfect. Events at Melbourne were entirely different. The "Osterley" was anchored well off-shore in Port Philip Bay. It was impossible to distinguish anyone waiting to greet passengers disembarking at Port Melbourne.

A general announcement was made that the Pneumonic Influenza Plague now threatened Australia with several cases reported in Victoria. For this reason, no visitors were allowed ashore. White cotton face masks were issued to all those persons who had reached their destination and had to be worn before leaving the ship. With all formalities and cargo for Melbourne dispatched by nightfall, we were once more on our way. All was well until we were in Bass Strait. A very thick fog - not a sea mist - enveloped us and heavy seas pounded on all sides.

Soundings were taken every half-hour, with the strident

fog horn blaring almost continuously. We didn't go to bed that night. The ship had a bad list and the constant thumping of the soundings rocked us ominously. At daylight we were just off the coast of Tasmania. Instead of going north we had been driven in the wrong direction. Great praise was given to the captain for turning us, in such adverse weather conditions, back on course.

The storm had also upset the scheduled arrival in Sydney Harbour. To help facilitate this, the servicemen were asked to assist the crew in transferring the Sydney baggage from the hold to the deck ready for unloading. Ted went on duty with a promise to Margaret Thomas that he would ascertain her luggage had not been overlooked but safely deposited - likewise our own. Margaret went down to the dining saloon for lunch (first sitting, we were second). During that time, Ted returned looking very perturbed. I wanted to know the reason. He said he had found all the luggage okay, but Margaret's was labelled "Mrs M Thomas, 7 The Domain, Sydney N.S.W.," I queried what was significant about that, never having heard of The Domain. It was just a simple address to me as it had certainly been to Margaret. I was deeply concerned when I realised from Ted's explanation that the poor girl had been completely duped. We felt we could do nothing to help. No legal address and from it's implication, there would not be a husband either.

To tell her what was apparent to us before she landed would be inadvisable. The "Osterley" was not the first "Bride Ship" out from England after the Armistice and regrettable though it was, there were many unclaimed wives. (A few days later we read an article in the daily newspaper to the effect that all abandoned A.I.F. wives were accommodated in a hostel pending a return passage to England).

Early next morning, February 22nd 1919, we passed through Sydney Heads. The sun was shining brightly - the scenery incredibly beautiful. The servicemen pointed out the beaches and places they remembered so well. The Pilot came on board and we moved slowly to Woolloomooloo, where we tied up at the wharf. Ted was anxiously scanning the waiting crowd of people as we stepped off the gangway. A woman rushed towards us shouting "Ted" - "Ted". She was his sister Ettie.

Close behind her was Fred, Ted's only brother (eleven years his senior), Ted and Fred had a very strong bond between them. There were five sisters in the family. Ettie was tall with a good figure. (In later years I learnt she had once been a model for the Berlei Corset Company). Fred was an inch taller than Ted but more slightly built. I stood aside while the happy reunion was made, after five long years. Suddenly Ettie exclaimed - "Where is your wife?" Ted put his arm around me and simply said "My wife Queen". To which Ettie replied "I thought she was one of the children!" - Not a very favourable remark. It was Fred who avoided any further comment by his suggestion that we walk to the exit. I was certainly aware of my short stature in comparison to the height of my new "in-laws". Our baggage was being forwarded to Dubbo Railway Station.

Ettie lived in Bay Street, Rockdale. She had prepared an appetising lunch, after which Fred booked a hire car, with driver, for the afternoon.

We were taken around and through the city. Elizabeth and Macquarie Streets remain prominently in my memory as being distinctive on that first visit. We went on to Darlinghurst, Bondi Beach, Coogee and then to La Perouse. We left the car and crossed by the footbridge to Bare Island - an ancient concrete Fort built in 1885 and full of interest.

We returned to Rockdale after a very enjoyable and comprehensive tour and had our evening meal. Later we talked about Ettie's husband, Syd Kitchen, who was still overseas with the A.I.F. yet to be repatriated, then to family details and of course Pine Farm, Dubbo.

Maybe my natural "British reserve" influenced Ettie in her attitude towards me. I had never found it easy to chat spontaneously. The conversation had been enlightening to me but referred to people and places I had never heard of, consequently I was not talkative. Whatever reason accounted for it, there was no accord between us. I just felt I had not been totally accepted. Fortunately Ted had no inkling of this and everything went smoothly. (My first impressions proved to be correct. Ettie was always unfriendly towards me for the rest of her life). Bed-time approached.

The house only had two bedrooms, each furnished with a double bed. There was no other item of furniture that could be used as a couch. No problems apparently. Ted and Fred shared one room and Ettie and I the other. I realised, miserably, I had to sleep with a person I scarcely knew and one who was not very congenial either. However, I was glad to retire.

We had been travelling just over six weeks from England and I had experienced a mixed emotional day since landing, which must have been conducive to my good night's sleep.

The next morning we went by rail to Central Railway Station. We left Sydney about 9am for Dubbo. It was a long slow journey, nearly 300 miles. We stopped at almost every station. At one of them we bought hot meat pies for our lunch. I was able to see many views of this new country. I was greatly impressed with the beauty of the Blue Mountains with glimpses of equally beautiful valleys. As we journeyed further, the effects of the terrible 1919 drought were very evident. Bare paddocks with cattle and sheep in poor condition. Ted asked Fred if "Pine Farm" had suffered badly too and was told there had been heavy losses. Fred had not mentioned it because he didn't want to dampen our home coming with bad news. Ted had suspected this from what we had seen.

The light was fading as we drew into Dubbo station. Before the train actually stopped, the engine driver (by some given signal) gave the "Cock-a-doodle-doo" blast on his engine whistle, very loudly, three times. Fred informed me it was my official "Welcome" to Dubbo, being the first War Bride in the vicinity. It gave me a great feeling.

Dubbo Railway Station 1919

A tall man opened the door of our box carriage. By the hearty handshake he gave Ted, I guessed he must be a special friend. He gave me a warm welcome too and was introduced as Tom Bowen. He escorted us out of the station to his car. I did not learn much about Tom or the Bowen family that night, except the invitation to meet them in town when we had settled down. Tom drove the 14 miles out to the Farm.

Fred opened the cyclone gate to the property - a short distance from the homestead. It was dark and I could only distinguish a low railing fence around the house. Ted took me through a little wooden gate on to a verandah with an open doorway, into a room full of people. He embraced his mother first. She appeared much older than her seventy-five years but was very active and so happy to have her son safely back again. Meeting her gave me an odd sensation, it was like meeting my grandmother. She said quite pleasantly she was glad to meet "Ted's wife". I felt she was conveying to those in the room that my status was accepted. In no time after that he was almost smothered with hugs and kisses - everyone clustered around him. Ted and I became separated. So overwhelming was their greeting and joy, I wasn't noticed. A door on the other side of the room was open so I passed quietly outside to another verandah. I had never felt so alone in all my life. "What on earth was I doing here?" Ted came looking for me and sensed my doubtful state of mind. He re-assured me in the nicest way - we did love each other very sincerely.

Among the visitors I met were two more sisters - Lily (Mrs Jim Green) and Clara (Mrs Aubrey Chater), with their families. Fred's wife May was kept busy but she had been warm and friendly.

The weatherboard building we were in consisted of two rooms with a verandah each side. A kitchen, separated from the dining room by a partition. The kitchen was not spacious. A big fuel stove, fire box above a large oven, in which yellow box or apple wood was split into suitable lengths ready to burn. Beside the stove was an open log fire space. This occupied one end. By the partition was a fair sized table. No sink and no water tap. Water was supplied by a long underground pipe connected to the windmill over by the horse yard. It was "hard" water, impossible to create lather and far too brackish to drink. The tap was on the verandah and a two thousand gallon rainwater tank was in position at the end of it.

The dining room was much larger. It had a pine table which almost filled the room and cane seated chairs - fourteen in number. On one wall was a wide open dresser, with drawers and cupboards and on the other, a Chesterfield couch. Above the couch was a window. It had a wooden shutter but no glass and was closed at night to keep out the insects attracted by the light from the kerosene table lamps. The floors were plain pine boards with no covering.

Before the party had ended, May offered to take me to our room. I had wondered where the sleeping quarters could be. We crossed a garden area in the light from the house, went around a big Kurrajong tree, past another two-room building separated by a narrow strip of garden from a second similar structure. Each had a front verandah and in the second one each room had its own front entrance. There was a central partition. One section was Mother's room, the other was ours.

The walls were built of wattle and daub, no ceiling but a galvanised iron roof. The walls freshly whitewashed. May had gone to a lot of trouble to make the ancient place as attractive as she could. There was a metal four-poster double bed, complete with valance all around and a fitted mosquito net. The bedding was white and all brand new with a honeycomb counterpane. The dressing table, with its upright hinged mirror, was surrounded with a pretty muslin frill. Curtains to match at the shutter window. Two new rugs on the board floor, a cane easy chair and a bedside table and candlestick. I was truly appreciative of her preparation and kindness, yet very conscious it was certainly unique compared to any previous bedroom I had occupied. The next morning I was shown the building near ours. It was slightly larger. The front door led into a sitting room, comfortably furnished with a door in one wall opening into a bedroom which was occupied by Fred and May.

On the verandah outside was a single "Tester" bed with its mosquito net on the half hoop iron frame above the pillow. It was being used by Myra Farley, age 20 years, May's younger sister from Sydney who was spending a holiday on the farm. This dwelling was also wattle & daub.

To explain the reason for the separate dwellings, I must give some family history which is a little complicated. First of all Ted's mother - Elizabeth Tarrant, born at Windsor, New South Wales, 6-9-1844. She married Thomas Jones and had nine children, all eventually died tragically. Three of them from Enteritis at a very early age.

Thomas Jones died from cancer. At the time of his death a son Tom, and a daughter Jane were still living. They were both single. Elizabeth Jones (Ted's mother) met and married Thomas Sunderland.

Jane Jones (the daughter) married Christopher Sunderland (younger brother of Thomas). Thus mother and daughter married two brothers. Both men were Teamsters. The son Tom Jones was drowned in a flash flood, when he attempted to cross the Macquarie River at the Minore crossing on his way home. There was no traffic bridge until 1903. Ted was in his teens when the tragedy occurred.

Elizabeth and Thomas Sunderland had eight children:- Mary, Lily, Fred, Linda, Ettie, Clara, Edward and Minna. Minna died in infancy.

Thomas Sunderland built a homestead across the lagoon. Their entire family was born and reared there.
When I came to the property there were no ruins, it had all been cleared. Ted was able to show me the exact spot because the old well site was still there. The girls (Ted's sisters) were all young when they married and left home. Fred married May Farley and stayed with his parents to work the farm.

I don't know where Jane and Chris Sunderland lived but they had four children. Nina, Christina, Arthur and William. Ted's parents took the four children into their home, across the lagoon, when Jane died about 1893. Ted's mother told me she had three baby boys eighteen months and under, to look after at that time. Arthur, Ted and Bill (besides the rest of her own family). I understand that John Sunderland and Granny Williams lived in two separate dwellings on the site of "Pine Farm" that eventually became my home.

Granny Williams (no relation) and her husband owned a few acres on the Coalbaggie Creek, near the river, adjoining Pine Farm. When Mr Williams died, Tom Sunderland bought their land and took care of "Granny". There was one daughter, Jane. She married James Sunderland, another brother of Thomas. Their children were George, Ettie, William, Annie, Harry (Mick), Lachlan and Matilda (Tiny).

They lived at "Iona" the other side of the cowal from Pine Farm. Jane died in childbirth, leaving a baby daughter Eileen. Ted's sister Linda adopted her. Unfortunately at the age of three years she wandered too close to a wood-heap bonfire and the frill of her little frock caught alight. She was taken to Dubbo by horse and sulky but she died in hospital from severe burns.

Back to February 24th 1919 - my first day on "Pine Farm". I offered to help with the usual household chores but May and Myra declined it and suggested Ted show me the farm. It was a hot day and I was glad when we reached the shade of the trees in the river paddock. The property consisted of 780 acres, so it took several days to get acquainted with all the paddocks.
The effect of the drought was very evident. All the sheep and cattle were in terribly poor shape and had to be hand fed. There was no grass and the stubble from the wheat paddocks had all been eaten. We walked along the top of the steep river bank (the water was very low) and on to the junction of the Macquarie River and the Coalbaggie Creek. There was a big old steam engine firmly embedded in the ground with a huge stack of thick logs beside

it. A large pipe extended down the river bank into the water which was pumped up to the adjoining lucerne paddock. It was dried lucerne from previous crops that was keeping the stock alive at that time.

Steam engine used to pump water
from the river to the lucerne paddock.

When we returned to the house Fred was busy making supports for the cows too weak to stand up. Ted went quickly to help him in the cow yard. I tagged along and was given the job of holding a wheat bag while it was being cut open on one side and across the bottom. Fred had cut some stakes. I held the bag while the men fastened a stake securely in each corner. It looked like a wide canvas stretcher on long legs. The bag was placed underneath the cow and the stakes were driven into the ground until the animal was able to stand at its own normal height, supported by the sling.

I had only been in Australia a few weeks when I was privileged to see a sight of a lifetime. We were just about to commence our mid-day dinner on this particular occasion, when Fred jumped up and bid us to follow him very quietly out to the front verandah. Through the open door he had seen some big birds (like large cranes) land in the paddock in front of us. The flock had formed into a ring and were dancing in and out with graceful and varied movements. They were Brolgas and seldom witnessed in their "coroboree" dance. They were never seen again on Pine Farm.

The days went by - Ted still helping me to get used to everything. May and Myra did not encourage me to spend any time with them. I certainly had no experience of housekeeping and the jobs entailed, but I was perfectly willing to learn. I spent a few lonely hours in our room when Ted was busy - making the bed and keeping the room tidy and clean and then reading.

One day Ted found me in tears so he promptly took me with him out to the front paddock of 100 acres. He was relieving Fred who had been ploughing since early morning. They were cultivating new ground and were using a "Stump-jump" plough, especially made for the purpose.

It had a long iron seat, I climbed up behind Ted and away we went, bumping over thick roots of broken tree stumps hidden in the ground and rabbit holes and burrows. Oh the dust!. It was a terrible ride and I felt weepy all over again. Ted told me to have a good cry as my tears would water the dry ground and would produce a bumper crop later on which would enable him to take me home.

I only saw my Mother-in-law (Grandma Sunderland) at odd times. She was a remarkable woman, a real Pioneer who was fiercely independent and at 75 was physically very strong. She looked after herself and the only thing in the house she did, on her own insistence, was to make the bread twice a week. The yeast was made from liquid in which potato and hops had been boiled and stored in bottles.

Other than that she would make her bed, have her breakfast, shoulder a wide blade hoe and go down to the lagoon paddock to chop down Bathurst Burrs and Scotch Thistles. Like the men, the sun was her clock. Meals were always exactly on time and she knew when to come back for the hot mid-day dinner. She had learnt to read and write in her young days with the help of an English "remittance" man. (A remittance man was a person paid by his family to stay abroad. He had probably been in disgrace and banished from his home).

On mail days - Wednesday and Saturday - Grandma would read the *Dubbo Liberal* from front to back page before returning to the paddock. The mail was delivered by a mailman who had contracted for the run from Dubbo to "Kookaburra" Station, some 20 odd miles. He also carried various items in the buggy such as farm requisites and grocery previously ordered from Dubbo. We had a fairly large leather bag which was placed in the fork of a tree beside the road of the mail route, about half a mile from the homestead. I had to wait ten weeks for my English mail.

Several items for the farm and some grocery were required and at the weekend, May suggested Ted take me to Dubbo, do the shopping and then visit the Bowen family. We set off on Saturday morning in the sulky. I was overjoyed to be active again with shops and people and possibly new friends to make. Ted was still in uniform - his official military discharge had not yet been issued. After a very dusty drive, we drove into the yard of the Exchange Hotel on the corner of Macquarie and Wingewarra Street and opposite the Royal Hotel. The road was badly corrugated from the loose gravel surface. There was a dirt track parallel with it along the fences of the paddocks called the "soft road" which made for a smoother ride but also raised an even greater cloud of dust all the way.

We passed several homesteads, the old Dickygundi Hotel, Whylandra Reserve, down Bourke Hill across the railway line and into West Dubbo, over the White traffic bridge, turning into Macquarie Street at the Bushman's Home. The Bushman's Home situated at the corner of Bultge and Macquarie Streets was built in the early 1880's and was known as the Imperial Hotel. Many years later it became a boarding house for old men. The groom at "The Exchange" took charge of our conveyance and fed the horse.

Macquarie Street was fairly busy. Most farmers came into the town to shop on Saturday. Horses and sulkies were usually taken to hotel yards. Some were pulled along the kerb with the reins loosely tied to the front board of the sulky. I learned that a buggy was a four-wheel vehicle of which there were several in the street. There were no cars.

Masonic Temple, Dubbo

There were a great number of verandah posts supporting wooden roofs over the pavement. These roofs afforded good shade for pedestrians and protected the displays in shop windows. On our way, we passed Mitchell's barber shop, with its red and white barber's pole outside, Alam's Model Store and the Blue Bird Bakery. On the opposite side of the street was the old Berrima Building in which was a butter factory with a butcher's shop next door. Ted explained that almost all the shopping for the "Estate of T. Sunderland" (as Pine Farm was officially known), was transacted with The Western Stores (later Western Stores & Edgeley's) on a one year credit system and was used by most farmers.

I needed some stockings and was shown the new fashion shade of beige. Until then, there had never been any other colour than black manufactured and the girl serving me was very definite black was now out-dated. Ted was highly amused when I paid cash instead of a charge account entry. I had never worn anything that had not been paid for - however I soon got used to the new way of shopping. When Ted settled the account at the end of the year, the Stores Manager, Mr J G Brown gave him a bonus gift of an elegant silver-grey velour Trilby Hat (also a new fashion for men).

While we were shopping, Ted met a number of his pre-war acquaintances. It took us quite a while to get from Macquarie Street, round the corner of the "Macquarie View Hotel" into Talbragar Street, past the Marcus Clark store, cross the street by Wilkins & Kennedy Coach Builders, into Brisbane Street, over the railway line, past the Flour Mill and Lou Anelzark, the wheelwright and on to the big rambling house - with an equally big yard - occupied by Mr & Mrs Tom Bowen and their three daughters (Violet aged 20, Flo aged 18 and Rita aged 16 years).

They were delighted to see us and gave me a true heart-warming welcome into their home and family, while Teddy, as the girls called him, was just as pleased to be in their company again. By the finish of the evening meal I felt I had known them all my life.

Mrs Bowen insisted we stay the weekend which we did. Until Mr Bowen had bought his sedan car to use as a Taxi, he had a Hansom Cab for hire. The big yard had stables for his two horses and a carriage shed. I was only two years older than Violet and I had much in common with the girls. It was a happy weekend and I went back to the Farm in much brighter spirits wearing my new tussore silk dust-coat. Ma and Dad Bowen (as they asked me to call them) invited us to return at any time we liked. They remained my best friends, my "Australian family" right through all the years.

The stores in which we had shopped delivered all our goods to the groom in the Exchange Hotel yard. He had packed them into the tray of the sulky under the seat. Easter came and Myra returned to Sydney - I never saw her again. May's attitude became very friendly after Myra had gone.

Ted's youngest sister Clara (Chater) lived about three miles away at "Hidden Lodge" near the Coalbaggie Crossing. She took Mother for a few weeks. Ted and Fred decided to have a fishing weekend at the river. On the Thursday morning before Good Friday, May did some baking and the men fed the stock and then fixed up their fishing gear. We had mid-day lunch as usual then loaded

the Dray. Fred drove us - it was drawn by a big
Clydesdale mare called "Gyp" so our progress was slow
and bumpy. Ted rode his horse. We proceeded to the
river paddock and pulled up near a rough little shack. It
contained a bed, table and a couple of chairs where the
visitors could leave any extra belongings they did not
wish to carry around. The shack also provided shelter
from the weather when necessary. Quite a few friends
came out from Dubbo to Pine Farm to fish or shoot ducks
and foxes. Some I remember were George Bell
(Proprietor of the Court House Hotel), Mr. Kingsmill (from
the Rural Bank) Arthur Cleaver (commerce), Alec Alam
from The Model Store and several members of the Police
Force.

The dray was unloaded and "Gyp" turned loose. May
and I took all the food stuff and extras into the shack
while Ted and Fred, each with a shovel, scooped out four
shallow trenches, a little deeper in the centre, in which
we were to sleep. A new wheat bag was spread in the
cavity and with a blanket and cushion our beds were
complete. Within a few feet of them was a huge fallen
tree already well alight. Our cooker by day and warmer
by night.

The men took their gear down the bank to the river. I
followed - full of curiosity - because there was no sign of
fishing rods and reels. In the water was a small rowing
boat. Fred drove a peg into the bank to which was tied a
strong green cord. There was another peg with a coil of
this cord wound around it, linking the two. Ted rowed
across the river to the opposite bank while Fred uncoiled

the cord as they moved, then drove the second peg into the bank after he and Ted had pulled the cord as tight as possible.

On the way back Fred tied short lengths of fishing line and hook to the cord at intervals which were soon submerged. Half way along they fastened a metal cow-bell to it, then more lines until they reached the first peg. The idea of the bell was to indicate when a fish had been hooked on any of the lines, its frantic actions would jerk the line and clang the bell. This saved numerous trips up and down the bank to investigate all the lines.

We returned to the camp where May had made a billy of tea. The billy can was a seven pound treacle tin with its wire handle over the top. The tea and scones were most enjoyable. It was a beautiful night, the stars so bright and clear. We sat on logs by the fire and talked. Fred and May wanted to hear about Ted's experiences and conditions in England. May was a different person after Myra left. We were good friends and got on well together. Our "beds" felt very firm and solid, but not uncomfortable, when we retired. We could all feel the warmth from the fire and after an active day we were soon asleep. During that weekend there were some hectic scrambles down the bank as the bell was tugged vigorously. The total catch was good (mainly cod fish and a fair size).

There were two long, deep water troughs inside the big horse yard for the draught horses. The water connected by an underground pipe to the tank at the windmill close by. Another underground pipe ran to another big trough placed in the shade of a cedar tree not far from the house, for the use of saddle horses and any visiting riders. The troughs were made from the trunks of huge trees and were about 18ft long and approximately 3ft wide. A strip was taken off the side to form the open top and the centre hollowed out to within a short distance of each end.

Outside, the ends were sealed against leakage with flat iron. A tap from the pipe supplied the water. Surplus fish caught at any time was brought alive in a wire fish cage from the river and put in this deep trough until we felt like having a fish dinner.

One morning I was lucky enough to see a small platypus emerge from a hole in the bank and scurry into the water. It was the only time I saw one. Ted and I checked the lines and then he rowed up the river to the beach along "Dulla Dulla", the adjoining property - another good fishing spot. Back to base. Fred was setting rabbit traps and as the mail was due Ted caught his horse and rode to the mail tree for the bag. Joy for me, a letter from my mother among the newspapers we received weekly - The Dubbo Liberal, The Referee, Smith's Weekly and the Sydney Mail. Everything was okay at the homestead although no doors were ever locked. Ted attended to the big Clydesdale stallion "Shepherd", who was kept in his own stable and yard, before he rejoined us.

I heard many stories the evenings we all spent together by that log fire. We had a few interruptions when the metal clang of the cow bell echoed down the river.

Tom Sunderland had been a horse breeder for many years and had sold some fine stock too. His word was his bond and what he said he meant without question. Ted recalled one instance when a buyer tried to beat the price down for two foals in the yard. Tom shouted "EDWARD put the rails up - there's no sale today". He refused to listen to the buyer's protests. Ted also remarked whenever his father shouted for him, he jumped to it at the "ED" before the "WARD" sounded - a very strict man indeed.

As a young boy, Ted said he was always hungry - growing so fast and big for his age accounted for it. The family meals were adequate and the children ate what was put before them - no eating between meals. To appease his hunger Ted got a billy can and unknown to his mother, would put several eggs in it and hide it down by the lagoon. (His mother sold every available egg as she had to contribute to the housekeeping money).

One of Ted's jobs was to go to the bottom of the paddock and drive the cows home for milking, after walking two miles back from school. On his way he picked up his can and filled it with water from the lagoon. There was always land being cleared by burning off dead timber and Ted would place his billy on some coals, boil the eggs hard and eat the lot. He was never found out.

Our weekend passed all too quickly. There had been plenty to do. The men had scoured the old steam engine and May and I had helped with the clearing and burning of stumps and branches in the paddock. We went back home on Easter Tuesday.

May's health was not too good. She told me while we were camping that she suffered from Bright's Disease. In our new relationship she was quite willing to teach me many things in cooking and housekeeping. I even persuaded Mother to show me how to prepare the yeast and make bread.

Shortly after, the Rawsonville people arranged a "Welcome Home" social evening to celebrate the return of Lieut. Lachlan Robinson, Sgt Bob Bootle and Gunner Edward Sunderland and his war bride. I wore a new white voile dress which had a black velvet belt, a full skirt with three deep tucks at the hem and white court shoes. It was not a gathering for adults only. Whole families attended as there was plenty of room for the children to play in the bright moonlight outside the old school building. Mother came with us. The men had built a huge bonfire at a safe distance and all the non-dancers congregated around it. I remember the coffee being made in a big copper by Mrs Balfour in the yard.

Inside the room the M.C. for the evening (I think it was Harold Harvey) asked everyone to form a circle and then I was led around and introduced to everybody. I couldn't remember any names at the time, there were so many other people besides Rawsonville residents who came from surrounding country districts. There was a good program - musical items and songs in between dances. Arthur Sunderland sang "Dem Golden Slippers" and the music was supplied by Herb Gephardt - accordion and Jack Wright - violin. Lt. Robinson (Lock) asked me to dance and as we circled the room we talked of Salisbury, England, where he had been in camp. Then, to my utter surprise, he said: "Do you know Lottie and Winnie Card, they lived at Harnham?" Of course I did and almost stopped dancing. He then went on to say he remembered meeting me very briefly at their home on one occasion. I had forgotten all about it until this reminder. It made my night. Someone here who had met me personally and knew my friends in their own home. I wrote to Lottie and told her all about it. An amazing coincidence.

We visited Ma Bowen again. Ted needed some time in Dubbo with his Tailor, Mr Harry Bear, who measured and fitted him for two new suits and two pairs of cream flannel trousers for cricket, ready for the day of his official discharge from the Military Forces when he could wear civilian clothes again.

The Sunderlands were all keen sportsmen. Before Ted was out of uniform he took me to watch a cricket match between Dubbo and Rawsonville. Cherry Langby was the Captain for Dubbo and Fred for our local team. They were the best of friends but absolute rivals at cricket. Fred was particularly anxious to win this match. At the last minute one of our country players was unable to appear. After a brief consultation it was agreed that Ted should be the substitute - one khaki clad figure among the players in white. To his credit Ted made 66 runs and took 3 wickets - hero of the victorious Rawsonville Club.

On April 29th, 1919 he received his Discharge Certificate, a very welcome document.

By this time the Pneumonic Influenza plague was raging in Dubbo and throughout the West. Many deaths were reported. May was not at all well and Fred wanted her to stay with her sister Nora in Sydney for a while and consult a specialist. She agreed as she felt I could manage to cope at the farm and look after Mother, Ted and Fred. (We managed quite well).

There were no telephones connected to country properties. If there was anything urgent, a telegram was sent out with the mail or to the people nearest to them. May left in June and I did my best to carry on. I made a few mistakes and learnt from experience. Everything had been so new and different. All the washing was done at the back of the house, in a big copper out in the open. The clothes were washed in a round galvanised tub on the rainwater stand, the big Tank affording some shade.

The long clothes lines outside the garden fence were supported by slender forked saplings for clothes props. Hard homemade soap was cut up and put in the copper but everything was hand-washed before being boiled. I starched all the linen (shirt collars, aprons etc) and hanging it on the line, I was dismayed to find big gluey blobs clinging to everything. When making the starch I placed the chunky pieces of the "Silver Star" brand into a bowl and poured the boiling water directly into it, instead of dissolving in cold water first. It was my first wash day ever.

Clara called in one day and suggested she take Mother to stay with her during May's absence. Some time later, I was alone in the house busy cooking when Mr Charles Wright Snr rode up on his horse. I answered his call and went out to the gate where he handed me a telegram which had been delivered with the "Dulla Dulla" mail that day. Mr Wright was an elderly gentleman and had done well to ride the distance - his hands were all at work so he came himself. I hurried down to the paddock where the men were splitting posts for fencing. Fred was very concerned and upset. He told us the telegram was from Ettie to say May was in hospital, critically ill and to come at once. We hastened back to the house. It was well into the afternoon and we knew the Sydney train left Dubbo at 6pm, travelling all through the night. Fred prepared for the journey while I packed his suitcase and Ted caught the horse and harnessed him to the big sulky. Ted and I had no time to change our clothes - we still had 14 miles to drive to the Railway Station. However we made it and returned straight home.

Our next news came the following weekend.
A telegram in our own mail bag from Ettie to say May had passed away the day after Fred's arrival and that the funeral had already taken place. Also the time of Fred's return.

I cannot describe the immense shock it gave us and we worried about Fred. We had to wait for further details from him. Ted and I went to meet him and was unhappily surprised at the change in him. We took him home but he had no desire to eat and was unable to sleep. He did tell us eventually that when he reached Sydney he went straight to the Waverley Hospital and asked to see his wife.

He was informed she was suffering from the Pneumonic Influenza Plague and being so contagious, no visitors were allowed. Fred wrote a little note to let her know he was not far away and asked for it to be given her. The next morning he was back at the hospital to make enquiries and hand in some flowers. He went to the office and before he could ask anything he was given a document. Fred couldn't remember whether the attendant made any comment for the document was May's Death Certificate. It was no wonder Fred was still in such a disturbed state.

The days that followed were extremely difficult and a great strain. Trying to ease the effects of bereavement and making little progress.
Six weeks later Fred took his own life. I will not dwell on that except to say it completely changed our lives. The shock to Ted was greater than that of anything he ever encountered.

I drove the sulky and we went to Clara to break the news to her mother. As we neared the house we could see Mother standing at the gate. I pulled up to speak to her when she looked up and said "It's Fred isn't it" and then walked away. Her grief very private. She had endured so much tragedy in her lifetime she sensed what had happened.

Ted could not accept all that had occurred so calmly. I realised and understood why. He was so recently discharged from the Army after four years of war and bloodshed. On Active Service he had seen some terrible sights and endured much himself. The impact never faded. Then May's unexpected and sudden death causing Fred's devastating distress, resulting in his last fatal action was just too much. Ted was still only 26 years of age. Not only had he lost his beloved bother but he had to deal personally with all the unpleasant circumstance relevant to it.

Being fully occupied was the best antidote. The drought had not broken and stock had to be fed. Quite a lot of fencing had to be replaced. We settled down gradually but Ted could not manage single handed.

A neighbour on the next property told us of a man who might be available to come and work. His name was Bill Hanchard. He was living in a cottage previously owned by Albert Cook, opposite "Iona" on the other side of the cowal. As we pulled up at his gate, he walked towards us and evidently knew who we were. Ted told him he was looking for someone to plough. Bill replied "Would a man about my size do? I'll see you in the morning".

Quite a new angle to me in engaging staff? Money or wages had not been mentioned. Bill worked for us for several months until the ploughing was finished.
We still spent the occasional weekend with the Bowen family and in turn the girls came out to the farm.
Ted's eldest sister Mary was married to Bob Green and

they lived at "Gentle Rise", a property at Mogriguy. Mary, like her father, was the only short-stocky member of the family but she was warm and understanding. She was also a good cook. They had a big house and a large family: Bill, Pearl, Robert, Ida, Reta, Ruby and Tom. They all made us so welcome that it was a joy to visit them.

With mother, we spent my first Christmas Day in Australia with Clara and family at "Hidden Lodge". Ted prepared a suckling pig and took it with us. Chater (he was seldom called Aubrey) had built a big fire with plenty of hot coals, well away from the house. The men put the pork onto a spit and roasted it. We sat on the edge of the verandah and ate our delicious Christmas dinner. Unfortunately for me, it was the hottest day I had every experienced - considerably over the century mark.

1920-1929

A few days later I was completely covered from head to toe with great red lumps. The irritation was beyond description. Ted took me into Dubbo for my first visit to Dr Alan Yuille in Brisbane Street. He prescribed Calamine Lotion and said my English blood was still too thick to cope with the heat of an Australian summer. My discomfort lasted three weeks.

Arthur Sunderland brought his wife May (nee Aldridge) and their little son Roy to visit us. They had a small market garden at Whylandra, quite close to the

Whylandra Crossing. Arthur was a lovable, humorous character and fun to be with. It was suggested, late afternoon, May and I should ride to the bottom paddock and bring the cows in. May would ride "Trixie", their sulky horse while Ted saddled up a quiet elderly "Tom" for me, on which I had been learning to ride. May was an experienced rider and carried the stock whip. We reached the 90 acre paddock at a walking pace. The gates were open, one on the lane side and the other facing the lagoon. May cantered down to the lane gate and then returned to me when she realised my horse refused to move beyond a walk. At her suggestion we changed mounts. I headed off for the lagoon gate and I did so, May cracked the whip to get "Tom" into action.

"Trixie" objected to the sound of that crack and started off full gallop. Fortunately we were racing towards the homestead. My efforts to pull Trixie up were futile. All I could do was sling the rein through my arm and hang on to the pommel of the saddle as she jumped over logs and water holes. I was petrified. Ted and Arthur were at the top of the hill and Trixie stopped as soon as she heard Arthur's commanding shout. I was wearing a tussore silk frock, shoes, but no stockings. The friction of the new leather saddle bruised my legs black and blue. That was my last ride!

One Saturday Ted and I had been to Dubbo shopping and called, as usual, to see Ma and Dad Bowen. Ma persuaded us to stay for tea. The three girls were absent. We had only just started our meal when Flo and Rita came home accompanied by two young men who could not be described as immaculate; for one thing, they both needed a shave. However, they were made welcome and joined us at the table. There was always a good supply of food. The visitors did not stay very long after Tea. Dad Bowen remarked to the girls that he did not mind them bringing the young men home but hoped they would meet someone less "scruffy" next time.

Flo explained that the men had been flying all day and looking after their machine and confessed she and Rita had paid them ten shillings each for a flight over Dubbo. The air men were Charles Kingsford-Smith and Charles Ulm on one of their barn-storming visits to Dubbo.

The terrible drought did not break until July. Arthur and May came to stay a weekend with us. Arthur was unable to work in his garden because of the heavy rain and visited Pine Farm to share in the jubilation of the end of the drought. We had an elderly man working for us at the time - he was only known as "Scottie". His main job was caring for "Shepherd". We still had the big Clydesdale stallion in his own separate stable and yard. He also chopped all the wood for the house and stacked it in its fixture outside the kitchen door. The men were enjoying a friendly game of "500" when there was the sound of a dull roaring. Ted went out on the verandah - he knew what it meant and called out "The Coalbaggie is coming down".

Since the Coalbaggie Creek and Macquarie River junction was the boundary of our land and the height of the river had risen ominously, it would not take long for the river to overflow its banks and flood our lower paddocks. There was also a natural "break-away" caused by the previous floods, near the neighbouring fence, which would carry water right to the lagoon from the swollen river. The sheep and cattle were in those paddocks.

Ted and Arthur donned their raincoats and hats, took their horses from the yard to the harness shed, where they saddled up and set off to bring all the stock to the home paddocks safe high ground. By the time this had been accomplished it was nightfall. Scottie had put the chaff out for the horses so the men only had to put their riding gear away and come and partake of the evening meal.

It was still raining the following morning but I could not resist going to the top of the hill and taking shelter under the roof of the blacksmith shed. The lagoon was full and had overflowed. There was water right across the paddock and around the base of the hill, on the slope of which were the pig sties and above them the cow yard and bails.

The rain stopped and in a few days the surplus water disappeared. Just as rapidly the young green shoots of the winter grass were visible. It was cold and frosty early morning and night but the temperature throughout the day was remarkably warm and pleasant.

We could now bring the young sheep, which had been some forty miles way since April on agistment because of the drought, back to Pine Farm. I stayed with Ma Bowen while this operation was carried out by Ted and a drover. On Ma's advice I went to see Dr Yuille. He confirmed, all going well, Ted and I could expect our first child in the new year. Ted was absolutely delighted at the news when he rejoined us in Dubbo.

We went back home the same day. As we unpacked our shopping etc., Ted gave me a bulky parcel. It contained six yards of white Voile, six yards of Viyella, a big card of lace and some baby ribbon.

Unknown to me he had shopped on his way to get our conveyance from the Hotel and possibly with the help of the salesgirl, had purchased the materials for the baby clothes. I gave him full marks.

There was plenty of work to be done. The flood water had washed big logs and all kinds of debris on to the fences and broken them down. Joe Druitt was working for us at that time.

At the beginning of Spring Ted's repatriation money was paid for his military service. We had been waiting for it to arrive in order to improve the homestead building. The heavy expense of the long drought had prevented using money for that purpose.

Wallace and McGee, a building and supply firm in Dubbo, delivered all the necessary items - the timber, corrugated iron, windows etc., to the farm. Lock Robinson kindly offered to help Ted with the construction and they built on to the existing dining room and kitchen, with a ten foot wide verandah on three sides of the new rooms. We converted the old dining room into a bedroom for Mother and made a sleep out section for ourselves at the other end of the verandah, outside the new front bedroom. We transferred the furniture accordingly and completely demolished the two wattle and daub structures we had used as bedrooms.

We slept outside the whole year round. Canvas roller blinds kept out wind and rain when necessary.

Pine Farm

Prior to the building operation, Ted noticed the rapid growth of the grass in the paddock below the stockyards and realised that during the heavy rain in July, the yards had been thoroughly flushed down, carrying the "fertiliser" with it, thus improving the soil on the level ground below the hill.

He got the horse and single furrow plough and cultivated the area which looked so fertile. He planted seed potatoes in the furrows and in due course we had a prolific result. I have never eaten potatoes like them, they were so good. Our supply lasted a long time.

During Ted's youth, the nearest neighbours were the Currie family. The friendship commenced then, continued right through the years.

Roy Currie and his sister May now lived in the house on the corner of the turn-off to the Rawsonville Bridge from the Narromine Road. Mr Currie Senior had sold the "Glen Isla" property next to "Pine Farm" to Mr George Robinson, who kept the wayside "Minore Hotel" (Officially "Dickygundi" when that area of Minore had its name changed 1902).

A son - Bill Robinson, his wife Annie and little daughter Freda now lived there; my nearest neighbours. Annie was daughter of Jim Sunderland, so was first cousin to Ted. Bill was an older brother of Lock.

The Robinson family:- Ethel (Mrs Lindsay), Olive (Mrs Char Forrest), Charles (wife Teresa), Opal (Mrs Oakey Bootle), Bill (wife Annie), Leslie (killed in action A.I.F.), Lachlan (single), May (Mrs D'Esmonde), Gladys (Mrs Jack McGrath), George Jnr (Thelma Cross), Sylvia (Mrs Dunkley).

Roy Currie was the local mailman and May, his sister, kept house for him. She was a brilliant pianist and Roy had a good light baritone voice. I remember on one occasion we had just finished our evening meal when Roy arrived and asked if we would like to share some music with his family. We readily accepted - no need to change our clothes.

Ted had to get our sulky harnessed up and off we went. Roy had invited us to drive in his vehicle and he would bring us home later. At my express wish we declined. Roy also broke in horses and this particular night he was driving a newly broken in horse in a breaking in gig, little more than a pair of saplings for shafts, two odd sulky wheels and a board seat. Roy, with his dry humour, had named the horse "The Yellow Peril" and such it was. It would start to rear up on its hind legs if the person did not open the cyclone gate quickly. Hence my fear.

A nice surprise for Ted when he arrived. Roy's elder brother Gilbert was spending a few days with them. Gil was a Fire Assurance Assessor and lived in Sydney. In the family were two more sisters - Lyn, who was married and Irene, a nurse. Both living away from Dubbo. We were soon around the piano. Roy favoured the songs of Peter Dawson. It was the first time I had heard "The Road to Mandelay".

May entertained us with such Compositions as "Barcarolle" and "La Paloma", accompanied by Gilbert on the violin. Music - not noise. This continued until the early hours.

Ted killed and dressed all our own meat. There was a

good variety - hoggett (yearling sheep), beef, pigs and poultry. After a few weeks of mutton we would ask around the neighbours if any of them were ready for beef. A bullock would be shared, with the neighbours assisting. When they killed, we would get a similar share back - no money transactions. The greater portion of meat had to be corned as there was no refrigeration. We had two big wine barrels with wooden lids. The meat was covered with brine, a mixture of coarse salt, salt petre and cold water.

All the fat was rendered down and clarified, then poured into four gallon kerosene tins. (A kerosene tin cut in half made an excellent bucket, the cut edge folded and hammered down, with a twisted wire handle completed the job).

When soap was needed and the fat solid, it was weighed on a steelyard and put into the copper with measured water and resin and boiled. Then borax and caustic soda was added very slowly and carefully because it bubbled up. The copper was kept gently on the boil for two hours. The wood fire constantly tendered accordingly. Our tea was bought direct from Bushell's Warehouse in Sydney - big three ply wooden chests with metal binding and lined with tin foil.

We took our own wheat to the Dubbo Flour Mill to be ground into flour. Sugar was also purchased by the bag. Milk was strained and after retaining (daily) sufficient for the house was put through the separator for cream - always a plentiful supply. I made all our own butter with a hand whisk and all our own jam, pickles and chutney. I also preserved fruit, beans and onions.

A folded blanket with a folded sheet on top of it was spread over the kitchen table for ironing the clothes on wash-days. Flat irons were heated on the top of the stove and you had to guess the temperature at which to use them. A thick pad was necessary to hold the handle, almost as hot as its base. Another cloth was required to thoroughly wipe the iron. Tiny wisps of smoke would penetrate through the lids on top of the stove from the wood fire and under the irons, which would leave a black sooty streak on the garment. The hot irons were rubbed on a large block of beeswax to keep them smooth. All the laundry to be ironed was damped and rolled down and packed into the clothes basket for some considerable time before being pressed.

The crops, wheat, oats and lucerne all looked very promising. There had been some good follow-up rain after the deluge in July and the stock were healthy again. By November, I had completed the layette for the Baby. Clara cut out the little garments for me and I sewed most of them by hand. I had an old "White" sewing machine which occasionally missed a stitch, so I only used it for side seams. I did tucks and a lot of hemstitching with lace frills. I also made bonnets to match. The petticoats had scallops for hems and were filled in with button-hole stitch. A January baby did not require much in the way of woollen clothes - those I knitted and Grandma Bowen (as we now called her) gave me a light Shetland Wool Shawl. We bought a large cane pram - nice and wide to keep its occupant cool, with a big lined hood. There were no bassinets around in those days so I lined the top half of a cane hamper. (These hampers did the service of a present day suitcase for clothes when travelling). This cane lid cover accommodated a full size pillow for a mattress with sufficient depth remaining to tuck in the covers. I only had to make two small head pillows for the pram and wicker cane basket. Incidentally, there were no handles. When the hampers were used for luggage, one half covered the other and was secured with long leather straps around.

The weather had warmed up with the temperature rising higher every day. The hearth fire place had been thoroughly cleared and the empty fountain polished and hung in the side of the wide chimney. The Fountain was a large 'urn-like' container. It had a lid on the top, a long spout and a tap at the bottom. It was suspended by a chain at the side of the fire so that we always had a good supply of hot water. It was too big to stand on the stove. During the summer months, I depended on a large saucepan to boil the water.

Christmas 1920 approached. I made two family size Christmas puddings and cooked them in pudding cloths which were hung up on hooks in the dairy until required. By this time I had really learned to cook. The men working hard out doors had enormous appetites. I baked cakes and tarts every day. A whole cake, be it fruit, ginger, sponge - whatever, would disappear at one tea-break. I made bread twice a week and always, the year round, a hot mid-day dinner.

We spent Christmas at Pine Farm. 1920 - Clara and family were our only visitors. It was extremely hot and uncomfortable.

1921

Grandma Bowen invited us for new Year and my 24th Birthday. She suggested it would be a good idea for me to come and stay in Dubbo. January 11th was coming up and with horse and sulky our only transport, I was too far from Doctor and hospital should a maternity emergency occur. Ted decided it would be better if I stayed for the remainder of my time in "Hopetoun Private Hospital" where I had previously booked in. Accordingly, I moved in on January 4th. "Hopetoun", as it was generally called, was a large two storey building with beautiful iron lace surrounding the eaves and verandahs. It stood on the corner of Brisbane and Wingewarra Streets (now the site of the Dubbo R.S.L. Club).

It was owned by Matron Munckton and was a general hospital as well as maternity. My date, January 11th, came and went. Our little daughter arrived at 4.40pm on January 19th, five pounds and twelve ounces. Perfect. "Rita".

The temperature in my room was 110 degrees. Matron, who was attending me, removed her cap and veil. Dr Max Yuille, who was looking after his brother Alan's patients during temporary absence, unbuttoned his shirt. I was not distressed.

On January 26th, then known as "Anniversary Day", Ted was playing in a competition cricket match in Victoria Park, Dubbo. During his lunch break he slipped round to "Hopetoun" to nurse the baby for a little while. He picked her up and within minutes she branded his cream flannel trousers right down the leg. The nurse on duty did her best to repair the damage with not a very good result. I suggested the quick purchase of another pair of pants - but not Ted. He returned confidently to the match and was met with teasing cheers from his team-mates.

I went home the first week in February. Ted had thoughtfully arranged for Ida Green, one of his sister Mary's daughters, to come and work at the farm for a couple of months. She did all the chores and I did the cooking.

Ida was very easy to live with and in her spare time did some beautiful crochet work. She tried to teach me but I was hopeless. (Years later it was a different story). Three weeks after I came home, Ted ploughed a good wide break around the house paddock preparatory to burning off stubble left from the wheat crop. He fastened a small burning log to the back of the plough and circled the area. It was a much cooler day with no breeze. The paddock was well alight when suddenly a gusty wind blew up, totally unexpected, and swept the flames across the break igniting the posts of the fence in the lane.

Across the narrow width of the lane was a 200 acre paddock of standing wheat, belonging to Jim Sunderland.

Fortunately the big water trough at the homestead was full and incidentally almost in line with the fire. Ted, Scottie, Joe Druitt, Mother Ida and myself quickly formed a bucket brigade and managed to extinguish the flying sparks and burning fence before it crossed the road into the wheat crop. Our kerosene buckets came in very handy. A nasty experience as there was no time to lose.

A few days later I was decidedly off-colour. Ted had to check the sheep in the river paddock and suggested he drive down in the sulky and take me with him, to be out of the house for a while. We had a new rubber tire sulky with a low chromium rail around the back. He harnessed "Jackie" in and off we went. We had received good rain falls and the grass was high. It concealed all the dead logs but Ted knew the track. Suddenly we hit a new obstruction and the force of the impact threw Ted out of the sulky as it bumped over the hidden log. One of his boots was wrenched off on the sulky step and he still had the reins in his hands. However "Jackie" had taken fright and he bolted, leaving me in the vehicle without any reins.

I heard Ted shouting "Jump out the back - quick - jump out the back!" The pony was galloping so fast I was terrified, I hesitated a second then turned, swung my legs over the rail and dropped to the ground. "Jackie" was still in full flight and an instant later veered into the paddock and hit a huge stump. The sulky, so Ted told me later for I was knocked out, spun the length of the harness into the air and crashed down into splinters on the stump causing the pony to stop. Ted limped along to

where I had fallen and carried me to the shade of a tree.
I soon revived and Ted was anxious to get me home. He
unharnessed Jackie, now completely quiet and rode him
bare-back to the house; he returned with him and the
big sulky to pick me up. The new sulky an absolute
write-off. I was shaken and badly bruised.

1921 progressed and so did our baby. As there was no
Baby Clinic or Doctor just round the corner, common-
sense was relied on but we had no serious problems.
In the meantime, Ettie had straightened out her affair.
During her husband's long absence at the War, Ettie met a
tall Welshman, Walter Jones and became involved with
him. Syd Kitchen divorced Ettie and she and Walter were
married in Rockdale, where Ettie was living. Syd also
married again later and had a family.

At Christmas time Ettie and Walter came to stay for a holiday. Walter was a Sign Writer and also a French Polisher
as a side-line. He was employed by Holden's Motor
Works (no connection with G.M.H.). Monograms on cars
was the current trend and Walter designed the monogram
and painted it on the car door. He also did Trade Marks
for various firms, such as the "bird's nest" on Nestles
Chocolate. He was very artistic. When he came to the
farm he was horrified to see us using a cedar wood table
in the kitchen. We had a pine table in the living room
and he exchanged them and set to work on the cedar.
The final result was incredible, the polish so smooth and
brilliant. It did not return to the kitchen.

1922

Rita was making good progress - she was now able to manage a few steps alone. Her first Birthday was near. Ettie made the cake and Walter iced it, in pink icing. He designed a road-side scene with a milestone in the centre, on it "Rita's first milestone 1921-22".

Grandma Sunderland expressed a wish to visit her sister Mary Packer who lived in Richmond with her daughter and son-in-law, Mr & Mrs George Silk. She proposed travelling to Sydney with Ettie and Walter when they returned home. Ettie could take her to Richmond, then she would travel back to Dubbo alone. Ted and Clara did not approve.

Clara suggested I should go as well. She would look after Ted and Rita in my absence (which was only planned to be a few days) and I could accompany Grandma home. This eventuated. On our first day in Sydney, Ettie declined to go with us to Richmond. Grandma and I found our way to the house and were warmly welcomed. We spent the afternoon with them and returned to Rockdale. The next morning we got the train to Dubbo. Grandma did not enjoy the city.

February 1922

The men were very busy carting wheat and the hot mid-day meal had to be ready on time. Rita was playing on the verandah and I slipped out to feed the dogs before the men arrived. Somehow Rita managed to remove the barrier we erected to keep her out of the kitchen. Grandma Sunderland was lifting the hot water saucepan when Rita toddled up to her. Fearing she might touch the oven door for support, Grandma hastily replaced the saucepan, knocking its base on the top edge of the stove and the hot water splashed over Rita's right shoulder and down the side. I heard the screams, as did her father and we were shocked at the accident. I undressed her and folded a pure silk wrap around her.

Ted brought the sulky over and we left immediately for Dubbo and Dr. Yuille. We travelled ten miles before we could pacify her. She then quietened down and did not cry or protest even under treatment in the surgery. Dr. Yuille never minced his words and this time I got the full blast for my carelessness with my child. Blisters, as big as twenty cent pieces had formed on her shoulder and chest, with scalding on her arm. When the dressings were finished, she was wrapped up in the silk again and Dr Yuille asked me to tell him how it had all happened. After hearing what had happened, he apologised for his language and said he always lost his temper when he thought a little child had suffered through carelessness.

Ted took us round to Grandma Bowen and she willing said we could stay with her as I had to take Rita for dressings every day for two weeks. Ted went back to the farm and collected clothes for both of us and brought them in. Grandma Bowen quickly made two little smocks for Rita with only the left armhole, thus protecting the injured area and the bandages. It was surprising how rapidly she healed without leaving any scars.

Towards the end of the year Ted was enduring a great deal of discomfort and pain from haemorrhoids. He had intense difficulty riding in the saddle. Christmas was near and Dr. Yuille prescribed medication for trial treatment to last over until New Year. Christmas was very quiet.

1923

Ted's condition grew worse and he lost a lot of weight. I drove him to Dubbo and had a talk with Dr. Yuille who said an operation in Sydney was necessary and that he would book him into St George Hospital, Kogarah. I wired Ettie to meet him two days later. She took him to Dr Graham of Rockdale and as his patient, Ted went into hospital the following day. It was discovered as well as the haemorrhoids, he had a "Fistula" in the lower bowel. This is a long pipe-like ulcer and consequently that section had to be removed.

Ted was very ill and Ettie sent for me to go to Sydney. I took Rita with me as I knew Ted would want to see her. He was so thin and pale but delighted to see us. He spent several weeks in hospital and then I took him home.

From time to time "Rabbit Trappers" would call for permission to trap rabbits on the property. We would receive a percentage from the sale of the skins. The trapper had all the necessary gear. An elderly man arrived one day in a respectable looking horse and sulky

- not the usual outfit with rabbit traps dangling from the sides and a lantern swinging at the back, but everything neatly stacked on the sulky floor. He was a good trapper and camped in the river paddock with his dog. After three weeks he settled up with Ted and decided to leave, saying he wanted to give trapping away and would sell his equipment. Ted bought the lot for a modest sum. The trapper humped his Bluey, called his dog and walked away. Ted polished up the sulky and with "Judy" in the shafts I had a conveyance all my own which I used frequently to visit Clara and let Rita play with her cousin Muriel. "Judy" was a quiet animal. She would only jog-trot at her own pace having been used to rough bush tracks with her pervious owner.

This suited me very well after my experiences with the gallop on "Trixie" and "Jackie" bolting with fright. Muriel Chater was a little older than Rita and she had not been very well for some time. Clara took her to the Doctor who diagnosed poliomyelitis (then known as infantile paralysis) and admitted her to hospital. She eventually recovered but was never very strong afterwards. In the following weeks, Rita became very listless and would lay on the chesterfield for long periods. The doctor referred us to a Children's Specialist in Sydney. Christmas was uneventful.

1924

Our appointment was early January. Dr. Childs diagnosed poliomyelitis effecting the right knee and leg and said she must not use it at all. He also added a sea trip would be very good. I wrote all this to Ted. Unknown to me, he accepted Chater's following suggestion that Ted should take us to England. Chater would move to Pine Farm as Manager and Clara could take care of mother. Chater was to send cheques at regular intervals to the National Bank, Salisbury, for our maintenance. When Ted arrived at Ettie's a week or so later, I got a surprise to see him and a much bigger one when he told me his plans. I couldn't believe I was going home. I went back to Dubbo the next day and packed our clothes, saw our Estate Solicitor and collected some outstanding money for our expenses on the voyage and returned to Rockdale in a couple of days. We still had to obtain our passports and a taxation clearance. All went well and we sailed the following weekend coincidentally in the "S. S. Osterley" of 1919. (troopship).

Ted carried Rita everywhere. We had a nice family cabin with plenty of room and a big cot. After a few weeks Rita began to show noticeable improvement. She regained her appetite and had colour in her cheeks. The ship's doctor said to try her for a short walk, then extended it every day. So good was her progress she was soon able to play with the other children in the ship's nursery. By the end of the voyage (seven weeks) she had recovered the use of her leg but had not regained her normal weight.

As the "Osterley" approached the English Channel we ran into a boisterous Atlantic storm. The clang of the water-tight metal doors as they were closed was un-nerving, all passengers shut down below. In the morning the doors were opened. The sea was still very rough with a heavy swell. The fiddles were on the dining tables - not many people were present for breakfast or lunch. I was really scared and persuaded Ted to ask the Purser for permission to disembark at Plymouth, our next stop. We could get the train to Salisbury.

Consent was given but we had to leave our baggage in the hold and collect it at Tilbury Docks. I packed all our belongings in the cabin and we reached Plymouth late the following day, still in bad weather.
There were two railway stations in Plymouth and to our dismay the taxi driver took us to the wrong one for the Great Western Line.

Eventually we got to the right station about 8.00pm and the last train to Salisbury was already standing at the platform. Ted dashed for the tickets and we boarded the train with only seconds to spare. We arrived in Salisbury at midnight, walked to Arthur and Lily's shop in Milford Street and to our relief lights were on in their residence above it. The door bell was quickly answered by Lily who was so surprised and excited to see us she went calling for Arthur and left us standing in the doorway, causing much amusement later. I had not seen Arthur since 1914 - ten years.

Arthur and Lily had been to a Fundraising Whist Drive at Harnham which had made them late home. They told us Mother and Triss Symons had gone to Tilbury to meet us at the Docks and were staying at the Tilbury Hotel. We left early next morning for Tilbury Docks (via London) where we were informed, due to a slight collision with a Channel Boat during the storm in the night, the Osterley would not berth until 3.00pm. We decided to go and look for mother and Triss at their Hotel, only to find they had checked out at 11.00am unaware the ships arrival time had been changed to 3.00pm. Not knowing where they might be we decided to have lunch in the Hotel Dining room. We had just been served when through the glass doors came Mother and Triss. Mother glanced briefly at us, turned away, then swiftly back again and called out "Queen"!! We were over-joyed to meet again after five years absence. Greetings over, we all had lunch and then walked the short distance to the docks. The ship sailed in on time. Ted arranged for our luggage to be sent to Salisbury and we left for that same destination, to stay with Arthur and Lily. Mother was Assistant Matron at a Ladies College in St Ann Street and lived there.

We spent a very pleasant time visiting Fred and Ad and Portsmouth and other friends at various places around Salisbury. We also spent the cash we had brought with us and when we should have been reimbursed at the Bank, nothing had been sent from Australia for us. We sent an urgent cable but received no reply. As it took three months for a letter to be written and answered, something had to be done. Ted decided to get a job to relieve the situation until we could contact Chater.

Although not experienced in anything but farm work, he applied at the local Labour Exchange for employment. It was now September and September the 29th was Michaelmas Day when all the Farmers changed hands.

There was a vacancy for a Farm Handyman at the "Home Farm". Idmiston, about seven miles from Salisbury and owned by House and Sons, Portsmouth. A rent free cottage was provided, with free milk. The wages were twenty seven shillings and six pence per fortnight. Ted went for an interview with the manager, Mr Jack Mould and got the job. We had to go to Idmiston immediately.

The cottage, I learned later, was built in 1623 on the corner of the lane opposite the Church, to accommodate the Monks. The thatch was approximately two feet thick. The front windows faced the road which led to the military Porton experimental Camp and were so small, a yard of 36 inch material, cut in half, made a pair of curtains. The front door opened into the kitchen - living room, which had a large low bay window, complete with window seats and looked out to a fair-sized garden. At one end of this room was a little passage with stairs to the upper rooms. At some time a room had been built on which we used as our bedroom because the ceilings upstairs were so low Ted could hardly stand upright. At the other end of the kitchen was a door into a laundry with copper and bath and the back door into the garden. We drew all our water from a well, winding the bucket up and down. Mother had sufficient furniture stored which she gave us to use. Continued letters to Chater brought no reply.

There were no shops in Idmiston, a Butcher in horse and butcher's cart called once each week, a Baker every second day and a Grocery van fortnightly. Ted's work was to whitewash the farm cottages and any running repairs, renovate chalk and flintstone walls, replace broken parts on farm vehicles and such like. He also cultivated our cottage garden and we grew all our own vegetables. There were also red and black currant vines and some gooseberry bushes. We lived quite well but there was very little spare cash by the end of the fortnight.

The garden was surrounded by a high wall separating us from the "Manor House" built for the owner of the property. As this was not required by House & Son it had been leased to Capt Mason who was stationed at Porton Camp. The couple who lived in the servant's quarters were Sgt Neb Harris (also at the camp) and Lottie his wife; she was cook - housekeeper for the Mason family when in residence. Lottie called to see me and she and Neb soon became our firm friends. We were all about the same age. It transpired the camp Cricket Team needed a civilian umpire. When Neb discovered Ted's keen interest and extensive knowledge of the game, he nominated him for the voluntary position. Neb was also the captain of the team which comprised two Lieutenants and the remainder were non-commissioned officers. Neb had a big Harley-Davidson motor bike with side-car. At the weekend cricket matches away, Ted would travel with the players in an Army conveyance, Neb would ride the bike, Lottie nursed Rita in the side car and I sat on the carrier behind Neb. It was our only recreation which we all enjoyed very much.

Christmas 1924 was near. Ted made a doll's bed with four posts and painted it in white gloss. It was Rita's

Christmas present and I made a complete bed setting. Mother produced the two big dolls she had kept from my childhood. Rita was delighted. Fred and Ad, with their three months old baby Barbara, came and spent Christmas with us and to Rita's joy the baby was able to lie in the new doll's bed. To describe the dolls for size - one was a baby doll with full layette including a tucked and lace christening robe and the other a French doll in street frock, hat and shoes and socks. Both of them had china heads and limbs.

The village school was almost opposite with a bell on the roof - it would ring at 9.00am, play and lunch times. Miss Ormiston was the only teacher. A very formidable person with a strident voice which could be heard from our garden. It intimidated Rita, she was unaccustomed to shouted discipline.

1925

It was very cold. House & Sons granted our request for a new kitchen stove which was damaged and inadequate. They installed a splendid new one, designed for the top plates to slide back and form an open fire.
We lived in that lovely old English cottage for eighteen months and were then transferred to a Farm at Andover, much to our regret. We were given the centre brick cottage in a block of three.

1926

This move was a disaster and only lasted four months. The owner, a retired major from the Army, Mr S Coward and Ted could not work amicably together as their personalities clashed. Ted was never subservient and unlike the other farm hands did not cringe or touch his hat before speaking to the Boss. This did not meet with Mr Coward's approval. They had an argument over some repairs and Ted decided to leave.

We went by train to Salisbury that day and quite by chance we met Mr White, the city rep for Hardy & Son (my employers of 1913) and asked him if he knew of any vacant flats. He directed us to 30 Chipper Lane, opposite the Municipal Library. The lady of the house answered our knock and after one look at us started calling out to her husband "Bob it's Ted come back"!

Apparently Ted had been billeted with this same elderly couple during 1917 and accounted for his sense of familiarity of the area. Mr & Mrs Uphill were only too happy to rent us the flat. We visited Arthur and Lily and my brother suggested we engage Pickford's the removalists to transfer our belongings from Andover to Salisbury.

I record this because I was so impressed with their efficiency. Two men with a big van arrived the next morning - we had not quite finished breakfast as we had not expected them so early. I had not even stripped the beds. The driver told us to leave everything as it was, go for a walk for a couple of hours and then return. This we did and when we got back the cottage was completely empty and the Van was ready to move off. There were no breakages and nothing damaged. They only charged us Five Pounds for packing and the seventeen miles removal to Salisbury.

During the time Ted was Umpire of the Porton Camp Cricket Team, he became acquainted with some members of the Maintenance Staff. He went to them and applied for work and was successful with a better rate of pay. A few months went by. Rita was five and had to go to school of which she was terrified. She was not at all robust and the effect of attending school resulted in a very reduced state of health. Her teacher, Miss Rooms, was very concerned and advised I visit my doctor and get a check up on Rita. Dr Gordon certified she was suffering from "Nervous Debility" and must not attend school until she was seven years of age. She also had to be given Parrish's food regularly.

Ted became unsettled and disturbed as to what could be happening at "Pine Farm" and I discovered I was pregnant, which didn't help matters - it was a very difficult time.

After a talk with Uncle Jesse, Ted sent another cable to Chater. If that proved useless, Uncle promised to pay Ted's fare back to Australia and take care of Rita and me until Ted had straightened things out. The cable read "Ignore this and you won't ignore me. Send one hundred pounds immediately. Edward". It worked - the money arrived speedily.

There were complications when we tried to book our passages. Because I was pregnant the Shipping Company (as did all Lines) required a certificate from a Doctor to say I was fit to travel. I approached Dr Gordon but he definitely refused to give one. He said my health and Rita's was too precarious for a long sea voyage. There was nothing we could do about it. Arrangements were made for Ted to leave as soon as possible. He got a berth on an old coal steamship the S. S. "Beltana" which went via The Cape. It sailed on 6th October. We went to London the previous day and stayed with Bro & Sister Frank Lindars for the night.

Rita and I went to Paddington Station to see Ted off on the Boat Train and not until it was out of sight did I sit down on a railway trolley and cry my heart out. Australia was so far away.

It had been arranged for Rita and I to stay in London for a couple of weeks to ease the parting with Ted. However I felt I wanted to return to Salisbury and get used to being alone with Rita. Accordingly I crossed London, collected our luggage and caught a late train to Salisbury. I received a post card from Ted nine days later posted on an Island off the Spanish coast. I knew it would be some time before I could receive a letter from Cape Town, South Africa, the next port of call and that did not cheer me up.

The weeks went by and I missed Ted more, especially as our flat was by no means convenient. Water and coal was brought up in buckets from the ground floor. Ted had asked Mr Uphill to do this for me. One very cold winter's day I needed both commodities and Mr Uphill was out so I went down the two flights of stairs, filled my buckets and climbed the stairs again. Unfortunately, the heavy weight I held in each hand (in my condition) strained the ligaments of my body. The result was from that time in December until the baby arrived at the end of the following March, I was unable to walk - I could only manage an awkward shuffle. It meant I had to have help. My mother resigned at the college and came and lived with me. My brother Fred made a special Morris type chair that could be adjusted to three different positions. I lived and slept in that chair for my last three months.

1927

In the meantime I did not receive a letter from Ted. No news of any kind over Christmas or my Birthday - a great concern for all of us and a very unhappy time for me. The silence continued until January 14th.

I am quite sure January 14th was the correct date that I received the long awaited letter from Ted. I read my bible daily and in the portion set down for January 13th was verse 5 of Psalm 30 "Joy cometh in the morning": My exclamation "If it only would" became fact when I received a very long letter in which Ted expressed the hope the letter he had given to a fellow passenger disembarking at Cape Town to post had duly arrived as he did not go ashore himself. That letter never turned up. Ted explained what a long trying voyage it had been.

The engines of the old S. S. "Beltana" broke down and they could only travel at half speed. He had been one of the passengers who answered the call for volunteers to help the ships stokers. Ted had written to me as soon as he reached Australia and he also enclosed a substantial money order. There was no Air Mail in those days and letters took so long by sea mail. I heard regularly after that.

Ted never told me what actually happened when he confronted Chater. He only said he had to be careful not to upset his mother who wondered why he had stayed away so long. She was entirely ignorant of the reason. Matters were, however, settled by Ted to his complete satisfaction.

On Thursday March 31st at 12.50am our baby arrived. She weighed 8lb 5ozs and had a cap of black wavy hair which she lost quite soon with fair hair replacing it. It was a bitterly cold night. Dr Gordon and the Nurse eventually departed, leaving my mother in charge. She was so busy attending to me, it was a little while before she checked the baby who she soon discovered was cold. I had been given a lovely bassinet on a stand - it also had a hood. Mother had lined it with mauve and white Broderie with curtains to match. She quickly packed two hot water bottles in beside the baby which speedily restored necessary warmth. I was tightly wrapped in a large bath towel by the Doctor - a procedure to get me mobile again. I was allowed to get up for the first time in the middle of April and after a few shaky starts I was able to walk again. My recovery was good and I began to feel

normal once more. Mother sent Ted a cable with news
of the baby on April 1st. Ted had sent our boat tickets
for our journey back to Australia during March. He said
how much he had missed us during the past six months
and booked our passages to avoid any delay.

Dr Gordon still had to give a certificate of good health
and this he was not prepared to do until the end of May.
He very kindly handled all the correspondence with the
Shipping Company and we were finally scheduled to sail
on May 28th. Daphne was exactly eight weeks old and
Rita was six year, 4 months. We had to say good-bye to
everybody at Salisbury because the train went right
through to the wharf at Tilbury Docks for passengers
only. One of the passengers, a very kind man about 40
years of age, helped us into the train and attended to my
overnight case. (My cabin trunk and baggage had been
forwarded to the ship days ago).

He even nursed Daphne to give me a rest while travelling
to the docks in the train. On arrival at the wharf, he
escorted me to the 'S' check point and made sure I had
all my papers in order. As soon as the ship's Doctor
approached me, he disappeared in the direction of the
boarding gangway before I could thank him.
I never saw him again.

I carried Daphne around the decks and saloons of our
one class ship hoping the youngest baby aboard would
cause him to recognise us again. Although the voyage
took seven weeks, there was no sign of him anywhere.
He must have been my guardian angel.

The ship's doctor briefly examined everyone before going on board. When it was my turn he said "You are okay, it's this baby I want to see. Where is the father?" I told him we were joining him in Sydney - he was very surprised and requested me to see him with the children regularly throughout the voyage.

One of the crew men took my hand luggage and showed me to our cabin. I was glad to lay Daphne down in the spacious cot after carrying her in my arms so many long hours. The cot was more like a deep bath like tub - no matter how much the ship rolled, the baby could not possibly fall out. Rita had the lower bunk and I had the upper on the opposite side of the roomy cabin which, to my great satisfaction, had a porthole. A Stewardess offered to stay with the children while I checked our places and table in the Dining Saloon. I was pleased to find we were at first sitting. I then went on to locate the Deck and our positions for compulsory boat drill. I also had to book and pay for the hire of two deck chairs for my exclusive use during the voyage. I knew I would need them for the girls daytime sleep, when it became too hot to stay in the cabin even though it meant carrying pillows up and down every day. How I missed Ted!!

I knew from previous travel that these things had to be done as soon as possible. To find locations early before the crowd was essential in my circumstances, as the number of chairs was limited.

To cope with the washing. I had collected old sheets and towels from everybody before we left England. These I cut up into squares (nappy size with no hems) and as they became soiled with use, I disposed of them very conveniently through the porthole. There were clothes lines on the lower deck which I used for other laundry and then pressed in the ironing room.

At meal time's I could not leave the baby alone in the cabin two flights of stairs down, so I turned her on her tummy across my lap during my meals. I was so busy taking the children up and down to the decks, doing the washing etc., that I could not participate in any of the passengers activities. no-one ever offered help of any kind except the stewardess and her time was limited. I had brought an enamel bowl in my cabin trunk, just large enough to give Daphne a bath. I drew the trunk out each day from under the bunk, placed a folded towel with the bowl on top and in spite of the rolling of the ship I managed quite well.

Two weeks after sailing, there was a baby show on deck. One of the mothers asked me if I had entered my baby. I told her Daphne was only ten weeks old and the next youngest competitor was seven months. She assured me that did not matter at all. It was very hot and Daphne only wore a singlet, her nappy and cream flannel pilchers - not dressed up to suit the occasion as I had only intended to be a spectator. However, I sat in the ring with the other competitors. The Ship's Doctor and another medical officer on board were the judges and they certainly gave the infants a thorough examination from head to toe. To my great delight and surprise the declared winner was "Miss Daphne Sunderland". She was awarded a certificate and a silver serviette ring bearing the S. S. Ormond crest. Daphne made no objection to being held in the Captain's arms during the presentation later in the week. I had dressed her in a pretty little frock.

It was not a good time of the year to be travelling. The heat through the Red Sea and the Indian Ocean was terrible. The humidity was so high, everyone's hair hung in wet strands. We eventually reached Fremantle but the Australian ports were of little interest as I had to stay on board. On July 8th we arrived at Woolloomooloo Dock, Sydney. I dressed the children in the new clothes I had brought for them to meet their father. We remained in the cabin when we berthed as there was too much activity going on to venture on deck. We did not have long to wait before being located by Ted, Ettie and Chater. After greeting me Ted went to the cot to look at his new little daughter. He exclaimed, "Queen, what a Beaut!" and picked her up. Rita had been very shy and tried to hide - it had been nine months since she had last seen him.

Chater had business in Sydney and had driven Ted down the previous day in his "Willys Knight" car. This was parked outside the wharf and after all my papers had been fixed up and baggage attended to, Chater drove us to Ettie's home at Rockdale. On arrival there, I was saddened to learn Walter had passed away in February from a brain tumour.

Chater left to keep his appointment before lunch. He

returned mid-afternoon considerably shaken and disturbed - minus the car. Apparently there had been an argument over some money transaction resulting in the car being confiscated. Whatever the deal had been, we were not told but Chater made no attempt to seek legal aid in the matter.

Instead of driving straight back to Pine Farm by car we went home by train, travelling all night in an uncomfortable box carriage. Tom Bowen drove us out to the Farm where I was surprised to find we were not going to live at the homestead. Chater had sold his property while we were in England and the Chater family were in occupation. As I now had a young baby and a delicate little girl it had been decided Clara should still look after Grandma Sunderland and relieve me of any farm duties.

A small cottage, two fair sized rooms with a front verandah and a lean-to at the back, had been built in the river paddock, completely furnished and included a large cane pram.

This was a big change from 1924. Many other things had changed too with motorisation. Chater had purchased a new car and Ted had a 30 cwt Bedford truck. Frequent trips to Dubbo enabled fresh bread to be bought regularly. No more home baking and no more butter making either.

A large market garden had been established between the lucerne paddock and the river nearby. A shack had also

Our Little Family
July 1927

been built on the creek side to accommodate the two
gardeners employed. (The Milliken brothers).
Ted delivered the produce to various shops in Dubbo two
and three times a week and supervised the garden. The
crops were prolific and lucrative. The rich virgin soil
promoted a good yield of tomatoes, onions, pumpkins,
cabbages, rock and water melons etc.

A single engine pump installed in the river supplied
irrigation and assisted the old steam engine, still useable
and later sold to a produce man on another property.
The Milliken brothers decided to return to Victoria and
left suddenly. Two more hands were engaged to replace

*Monty the old lorry
Load of Onions, Daphne, Ted & Rita,
Arthur Sunderland, Driver*

them. Frank Carswell, a well educated remittance
Englishman and Jim Holden an elderly Irishman. They
soon learned how to use a hoe and attend to the
irrigation. I cooked their meals.

1928

The wheat and garden crops were very good. Ted did all
the carting in his lorry. I still visited Grandma Bowen
with the children from time to time. She was a good
needlewoman and loved to make pretty voile frocks for
Rita and Daphne. Rita was now seven years old and had
to start school at Dickygundi on the Narromine Road.

Our neighbours children, Harry and Joyce Robinson, rode their horses and it was arranged for Rita to ride behind Joyce on a big brown gelding. Bob Condon was the school teacher.

Daphne had her first birthday March 31st. She was not crawling or walking but would pull herself up by a chair. No inducement of any kind of further movement met with any success. Daphne was quite happy in her own way. I became concerned and consulted Dr Yuille. He assured me there was nothing to worry about as Daphne was a heavy child and would walk when she was ready. Eventually, at the age of one year and five months, she took her first steps and rapidly gained confidence after that.

During October, Muriel Chater was admitted to the Dubbo Isolation Hospital suffering from scarlet fever. Clara and Chater visited her regularly so that she could see them through a window. On November 7th they called to see if I needed anything from Dubbo, not knowing Ted had already gone there with a load of vegetables. At the Court House Hotel, George Bell, (the proprietor) remarked about the terrible car accident on the Narromine Road and asked Ted if he knew the Fraters involved. Ted had a dreadful premonition and said, "Was the name Frater or Chater?" George was not sure and Ted phoned the hospital immediately and was told it was Mr & Mrs Chater. He went straight to the hospital.

Apparently while driving to town, Chater attempted to pass another car in front of him and in the thick cloud of dust did not see another car approaching. There was a head-on collision. The oncoming car was carrying two four gallon cans of petrol as the driver was a commercial traveller on his way out-back and needed to take the fuel with him. The petrol ignited on impact and Clara was tossed into the flames. Her entire clothing was completely burned from her body before the traveller could reach her, his arms having been injured. Chater was pinned under the steering wheel. The car he had intended to overtake was well ahead, quite unaware of the accident behind them through the dust screen and disappeared from sight. Another car from Narromine came along and its occupants were able to rescue them and convey them to Dubbo Hospital, covering Clara with a coat.

The tragedy was made worse by the fact Clara remained fully conscious all the time. When Ted reached her bedside only her eyes and the tip of her nose was visible through the bandages. She knew Ted was there but she was in great pain. Dr Yuille was standing by and assured Ted there was nothing more he could possibly do for her. The flames had destroyed her body. Clara passed away at 3.00pm.

Chater was in a stable condition. His chest had been crushed but he had been informed of his bereavement. A hospital sister took care of Muriel.

Back at the Farm it was mail day. The mailman now called to the house. He arrived about 2.30pm and related news of the accident. Chater had a very pleasant young man, Syd Percival, working for him on the tractor. Syd informed Bill Robinson, (the neighbour) and Bill quickly drove in his sulky down the paddock to tell me and also to take me up to the homestead to be with Grandma Sunderland. Daphne was in bed recovering from the measles. I wrapped her up in a blanket and when we got to the house Syd had Cath, (Clara had three children, Catherine, Muriel and Aubrey) and Aubrey ready to go to Dubbo with him and Bill Robinson. Ted was still very shocked when he got home later in the day and had to tell us of Clara's death. Grandma Sunderland was wonderfully calm - she quietly said "God's Will be done".

There were no tears, she had been tragically bereaved so many times, she accepted yet another with outward serenity and kept her grief privately to herself. She did not wish to attend Clara's funeral the following day, for which Ted had made all arrangements in Dubbo. I think she needed some time alone. Ted went to the River Cottage and collected necessary items. We never lived there again.

Chater remained in hospital.
Muriel was discharged from the Isolation in December, a very busy month with harvesting the wheat and oats and marketing the garden crops of early tomatoes and watermelons in particular.

On December 16th, I noticed a definite red rash on Rita's chest and arms and it did not take long to realise she had contracted scarlet fever. Whether the clothes Muriel brought home from the hospital had not been properly

Syd Percival, 1928

fumigated remained a query. We took Rita to Dr. Yuille straight away and he confirmed the symptoms. She was admitted to the Isolation Hospital. Just one week later, December 23rd, Daphne developed the same symptoms and she joined Rita in the Children's Isolation.

We could only peep through a window when we went to visit them and could only stay long enough for Rita to see us because we had been asked to avoid recognition by Daphne as she was fretting. She was one year and nine months old.

Trouble too with Rita!! The Sister in Charge told us Rita had a great fear that if she did not see me every day something must have happened to me the same as it did to Muriel's mother and she became very distressed until I appeared at the window.

117

We had not realised how the impact and shock of Clara's sudden death had affected our little girl so deeply.

In view of this report, I went in the horse and sulky every day (driven by Ray Taylor - a farm hand) to the hospital for six weeks. Ted was needed on the farm. Rita's bed was placed beside Daphne's cot which gave Daphne some source of comfort.

Christmas was not much of a celebration. We were feeling so depressed without our girls and yet at the same time had to do our best to make up for all that had happened to Clara's children, who now depended on us. Santa came as usual and perforce had not forgotten our two little ones, whose filled stockings remained tied to the foot of their beds, fastened there overnight by their cousins, now pleased with the result.

1929

Our girls were discharged from the hospital at the end of January. I now had five children, Grandma Sunderland and the farm hands to look after and cater for.

The wheat and oats safely harvested, there had to be a settling up of accounts between Ted and Chater. At that time the Police checked and collected all farm records throughout the district. Chater was still in hospital but had sent a request to Sgt Sweeny to check the Pine Farm figures on his behalf. The Sergeant duly arrived and it was evident he expected to find some discrepancy. There was none on Ted's reckoning and he was able to convince the Police officer by revealing the cash received for the sale of some seed wheat to the Robinson brothers had not been included in Chater's total calculation. Ted decided while Sgt. Sweeney was there on this specific occasion and commission, to verify all the farm accounts and get the record straight.

The end result was a settlement with Chater in Dubbo when he left hospital and it was significant Chater never returned to the Farm. I looked after his children for nine months and then he bought a small property for a market garden at Gilgandra, collected his family and departed. We never saw Chater again.

Our little cottage near the river was carefully demolished and the timber used for an extension to the gardener's shack. Frank Carswell, who was not very satisfactory in the garden, went back to Sydney. The Irishman, Jim Holden, came to the homestead to be general help with all the odd jobs, such as chopping and stacking wood for the stove, filling the Fountain to keep up the supply of hot water. He also did the washing up. Our receptacle for washing up was a four gallon kerosene tin, cut diagonally and the two sections securely nailed to a strip of wood each end for support and forming one division for washing and the other for drying. A piece of soap in a wire container was used for detergent.

Jim was a great tea-drinker and all day long there was always a cup of tea ready. He had no home and no relatives but was conscientious and reliable and was very fond of Rita and Daphne. He would continue steadily with his work for four or five months, without a break of any kind, then suddenly he would start using and eating salt! This was a definite indication that a visit to Dubbo would soon be requested. He would wear a reasonably good navy suit and walk to the road where he had no difficulty in obtaining a lift into town. He never asked Ted but would just disappear. His spree at the "Exchange Hotel" would last a few days, then Ted would go and bring him home and help him to recover.

For the record Jim had his own names for the girls. Rita was "Lucy Clitters" and Daphne was "Miss Chipperfield". I have no idea why!

The gardeners were replaced. Arthur and May Sunderland, with their son Roy, sold their small market garden at Whylandra and moved into the new river cottage on a 'Share Basis' with Ted, at the same time

Tom Bowness

Ted and John Saul (right) at Pine Farm

bringing Arthur's man Bert Bracegirdle with them. The area of the garden was extended to grow larger and more varied crops.

Ted was now able to return to farm work. He engaged two young Englishmen who had emigrated to Australia for an out-door life. Tom Bowness wanted to learn general farming and raising stock, while John Saul concentrated on soil conservation and land valuation whenever possible. He had been educated at Blundell's College - London but willingly accepted any job.

In later life they were both very successful. Tom Bowness became a cattle buyer at the Dubbo Abattoirs for the Ganarrin Meat Company and John Saul became a land and property Valuer for the Commonwealth Bank. Tom married late in life; there were no children. John married Gloria Price, the daughter of a Bank Manager in Bathurst and they had one son.

Close to the homestead at the side of the paddock was a large area of 'scalded ground'. Absolutely nothing grew on the hard smooth surface. Before the harvest began, Ted had the brilliant idea of using this bare ground for two tennis courts. The high wire netting fence around it was erected, two nets and posts purchased and installed complete with the Umpire's stand and seat.

In that era, tennis court lines were only marked with "white-wash" and needed constant attention. To avoid this Ted and the men gauged shallow trenches along the markings, filled them with a white content in the cement and we had permanent lines that only needed sweeping occasionally. Ted also built a shed alongside where the teams could sit in the shade and enjoy picnic lunches. There had been a lot of dissension in the local club on the Rawsonville courts, chiefly in grading the players, so we decided to form our own club and restricted the number of members. We were quickly dubbed, friendly enough, "The Breakaways" so we accepted the name.

The Rawsonville Soldiers Memorial Hall was built by Charles Carret & Sons. The building was finished and the Opening Ceremony was conducted by Mr Les Clark of "Dulciedene". Funds for the cost of the Hall were entirely raised by local effort. The committee for the project divided into four groups and each group in its own area tried to collect the largest sum of money. We had raffles, guessing competitions, garden parties and cake and home made preserves stalls. My contribution was always sponge cakes and cream puffs.

Mrs Cecil Harvey organised our group and functions were held at "Enterprise". On one occasion Ted obtained the loan of a chocolate wheel and collected various things for prizes for winning numbers. There was a very good attendance but after a while the wheel lacked players for a spin. To liven things up, Ted announced he would buy the entire book of tickets. This amused the folk and caused them to gather round, curious to see what Ted's prize would be. The wheel finally stopped, the winning number checked and the prize was "A pair of turkeys - donated by Mr Ted Sunderland - himself"!!

It caused a lot of laughter but interest in the wheel had been revived and it was soon spinning again with the pair of turkeys still one of its prizes. In the 1929 era, a poultry dinner was a decided luxury and very few farmers raised turkeys.

The annual Dubbo Show was held during the time I had all the children. Always an occasion for new frocks. I made floral ones, exactly alike for the girls and a new outfit for Aubrey Jnr. A couple of days before the Show opened the old "White" sewing machine broke down completely and I still had some sewing to do. Ted managed to coax it into action again on several previous occasions but this time nothing worked. On a recent visit to Dubbo, I had noticed an entirely different sewing machine - the latest model in the showroom of Bebarfald's Furniture Store on the corner of Macquarie and Wingewarra Streets. It had a drophead enclosed in its own cabinet with blue glass leadlight doors, which concealed the belt, wheel & treadle (all had been fully exposed in my old machine).

I had told Ted all about it, knowing my ancient model would soon pack up. So, it was into the lorry and off to town to Bebarfald's. The top salesman attended us and tried to persuade us to buy another similar model which had plain panel doors instead of the more attractive leadlight, which I definitely preferred. Apparently this machine was to be on display at the forthcoming Dubbo Show. The salesman was so persistent it annoyed Ted, who suggested to me we should go and see what Singer's had to offer. Very smartly the salesman changed tactics and cheerfully sold us the "Bluebird". Incidentally there was another "Bluebird" at the Show, obtained from their store at Orange.

Local communication had improved. A Party Line telephone, linking properties together, had been established. Each owner had their own individual Morse Code signal to identify them. In our case it was a "long-short-long" bell-ring 302K. There was one disadvantage - there were no private conversations. No matter what signal bell ring was made, anyone on the Party Line circuit could lift their receiver and "listen-in" which was actually practiced by some of the curious locals. Dubbo and Narromine exchanges were connected but no link with Sydney.

This was the year of The Great Depression when so many

people suffered so many hardships, shortages, loss of jobs and high cost of living. Farmers were fortunate. As far as our family was concerned we were scarcely affected. We grew our own fruit and vegetables, had plenty of milk, cream, eggs, poultry and meat. The only difference it made to us was the drop in the wheat and wool prices. My friends in Dubbo, the Bowen family, were having a hard time. Dad Bowen was not the only Taxi-driver in town, there were several others now and they all felt the pinch. People just could not afford to hire them and none of them could earn enough for an adequate income.

To overcome their difficulties, the Bowen family moved to a more convenient area - a house in Church Street, No. 74. Grandma now had accommodation for four boarders and with her tariff less than hotel charges, she had her quota in no time. There was a Mail Officer, a Bank clerk and two Railway Guards. Whenever a vacancy occurred it was quickly filled by another railway employee. It worked out successfully in every way.

1930-1939

General interest in the game of cricket had been increased considerably. A young man, Donald G Bradman who played for the St George Cricket Club, Sheffield Shield and interstate matches, had been making very high batting scores - many times over the century. He had now been selected to play for Australia in the Team currently in England to try and regain "The Ashes". By this time Radio had been established in Dubbo and quite a number of Dubbo residents had their own sets and were able to receive transmission from 2FC in Sydney. The cricket Test Matches in England were to be Broadcast in detail.

Ted had to go to Dubbo in the afternoon previous to the first Test. He phoned to ask Lock Robinson to organise the erection of two very high posts between the house and the woolshed, to be connected at the top with copper wire.

Ted had purchased an S.T.C. radio set, and an aerial was required. The men went down the paddock, cut two very tall saplings and soon had them in position. It was almost dark when Ted returned but between them, the men managed to find the wood and fix two shelves in one corner of the living room, one above the other. The set operated on three 'wet' batteries and two 'dry' ones, which had to be placed separately on these shelves. (very unsightly!!).

The set was placed on the top shelf and was turned on by an ordinary light switch. There was whistling and crackling from time to time but on the whole the reception was very clear. Together with the men currently on the property, we eagerly awaited the commencement of play in that first Test Match. Normally everyone would be preparing for bed but no such thoughts were enter-tained.The commentators at 2FC gave an excellent ball by ball description, complete with all sound effects realistically executed in the studio by Alan McGilvray.

The news spread very quickly in our locality. Ted

Sunderland had a radio set and could get the cricket. By
nine o'clock the second night, there were a number of
horses tied up to any available post outside our house,
their owners eager to listen to the broadcast. Seating
accommodation was a problem with not enough chairs
for all the visitors. However we managed with tomato
cases, a long stool from the verandah and some butter
boxes turned upside down. These boxes were very
strongly made of pine wood, about 18 inches square and
the timber nearly half an inch thick. They could be used
for many purposes as they were so smooth and nicely
finished off. Our new radio and battery shelves, in all
probability, was once a butter box. Our grocery from the
Western Stores was always packed in them, hence our
supply.

Roy Ford (the local school teacher) and his wife Nora
became great friends of ours. I was very glad of Nora's
help when midnight came around at these cricket
gatherings. We all enjoyed a cup of tea together with
cake and scones. This meant extra to the daily farm
meals. On one occasion during the Test Series, I had a
very heavy day's work and by 9.00pm I felt terribly tired
and weary.Refreshment had been served as usual at midnight and the cake tins were empty.

At 2.00am someone had the bright suggestion to boil the
billy again. Nora and I repaired to the kitchen where I
decided a "Victoria" sponge cake would be the quickest
cake to make. There was no "Mix-master" (they had not
been invented), nor did we have electricity.

The eggs and sugar were beaten together with an
ordinary dinner fork. (I did have a wire whisk later).
The cake was cooked splendidly, I blended an icing with
(as I thought) icing sugar, butter and vanilla essence,
spread it liberally over the top and between the two
sponge layers. Nora attended to the tea and I handed the
cake around. To my dismay everyone was making queer
noises and pulling faces as they began eating and for very
good reason. I had mistaken Baking Soda for Icing Sugar.
How weary can one get?!

Australia won The Ashes on that tour. Bradman scored
236 runs at Worcester, 185 not out at Leicester and 252
not out at The Oval. A total of 974 runs in the Test
matches and 2960 on the Tour. I quote these figures to
illustrate how exciting the cricket broadcasts were.

Later in the year I had quite a bad scare. The men were
harvesting and had come in for their hot mid-day meal.
The draught horses had all been shut in the horse yard,
about fourteen all told, to feed from their troughs. I was
busy serving the food when I noticed Daphne's absence
and a few minutes passed before I could go and look for
her. No sign or answer to my call and then I spotted
something white in the horse yard way up from the
house. I ran to the yard and there sitting astride the
biggest Clydesdale mare (which was named "Big Kate")
was Daphne, her back was towards me. In bare feet she
had climbed the high rails and dropped down onto
"Kate's" back, her little legs were not long enough to
reach right across but she was energetically kicking with
her heels to try and get some action. I realised instantly I

was powerless to do anything. If I called I might startle her and cause her to fall from her precarious position. I was too timid to go near the horses and too short in any case to lift the three and a half year old down. I ran hysterically to the house to get Ted. He insisted I remain indoors while he walked quickly to within a few feet of the horse yard, he then called out "Are you having a good ride. I'll come and get you now because it is time for dinner".

He also made sure she understood she must never go into the horse yard again by herself. Afterwards, when I had calmed down. Ted related these details to me.

Quite frequently following this incident he sat Daphne in front of him on his saddle horse "Jeanette" and off they would canter around the paddocks.

1931

The Druitt family had sold their property "Mt Druitt" to Jim Hopkins, only son of Mr Charles Hopkins of "Oxlea" Whylandra on the Narromine Road. Jim was a bachelor and chose to live in the old building behind the brick house which had been rented to our friends as accommodation for the school teacher, Roy and Nora Ford.
When the Druitt's were still in residence, Lizzie and Annie Druitt conducted the local sub-Post Office. A request had been published for an offer to continue this service to the locality. For our own convenience as well as others in the area I agreed to take on the duties of Post Mistress. Ted built a "lean-to" room on the side of the big garage

in which to operate the new project. A Mail Officer from the Dubbo Post Office brought the postage supplies and the equipment and gave me the necessary instruction to handle Post Office procedures.

1932

Ted fixed up a cubby house for the girls at the back of this new addition.

It was a very hot summer. As frequently happened, we all went to Dubbo on Saturday afternoon. On one such occasion we did so and met up with Roy and Nora Ford and little son Jack and made our way to Nick Brown's cafe, "The Golden gate" in Macquarie Street, for cool drinks (usually iced coffee) and ice cream. Daphne asked for a glass of cold water (her normal routine following ice cream) and before we left the cafe, Nora and I had also shared it.

The next morning I noticed an ominous rash on my arms and chest and recognised it immediately as scarlatina. Ted took me to Dubbo only to find Dr. Yuille was away on holiday and Dr. Hurrey was attending his patients in the meantime.

During the drive into town the rash faded from my arms (I wore a sleeveless frock). We disturbed Dr. Hurrey's Sunday dinner and he was quite sceptical when I apologised for the interruption but said I though I had scarlatina. He examined my arms and shook his head. I showed him my chest and he was all action immediately and directed us to proceed to the Isolation Block at the Hospital. This was opened by the time we arrived as there were no other infectious cases at all. I was given treatment without delay with a big injection of a new serum. Unfortunately, this caused a total skin allergy. For three weeks I was very distressed and the irritation indescribable. Strangely enough, I was the only scarlet fever patient during the whole period and although the same glass of water had been shared at the Cafe, no-one else contracted it.

Ted sold the Chevrolet lorry and bought a much larger International truck. With Tom Bowness to help him they secured a heavy gauge wire mesh frame right around and behind the cabin and also made partitions to use when loading sheep and pigs

The Ganarrin Meat Company, through Mr Stan Wilkins, a senior member, gave Ted authority to buy stock and deliver it to the Ganarrin Abattoirs. Tom Bowness assisted Ted and together they had a very busy time. Both of them were well experienced in judging the condition and weight of cattle, sheep and pigs and assess their market value, thus a fair offer in cash would be made and the deal concluded. Farmers from a wide radius would ring up and state the stock they had for sale and as there was no other competition, they were kept busy.

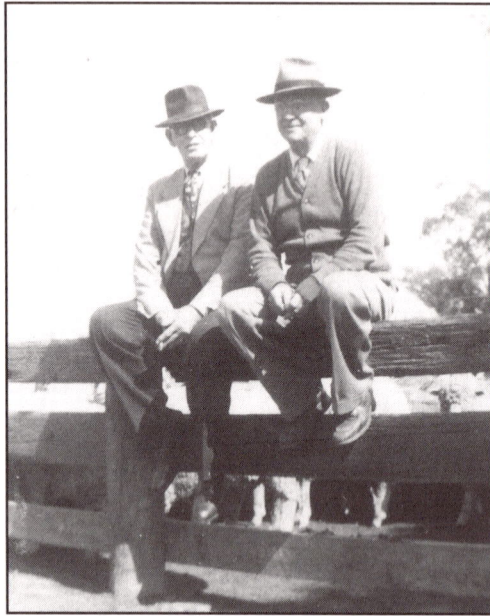

Ted and Stan Wilkins (right)
Buying stock for the Ganarrin Meat Co.

Load of wheat stacked by Ted
on our International

The Robinson brothers continued with the share-farming. During harvest, the filled bags of wheat were stacked in groups in the paddock being stripped. A man especially employed for the work used a big curved needle and twine to sew them up before they would be carted away to the Silo at Minore Railway Siding. Later the needle and twine was replaced by metal clips. This was a much quicker procedure and allowed the extra man to be dispensed with, any farm could do the job on their own account.

Arthur and May decided to leave and move to Dubbo. Bert Bracegirdle elected to remain with us and take full control of the garden and moved into the River Cottage.

Rita had her 12th Birthday which meant she had to attend the Dubbo High School. Grandma Bowen kindly agreed to board her from Monday to Friday for thirty shillings per week. We brought her home for the weekend and Stan Wilkins took her back on Monday morning with his son Darvall, also at the High School.

Our tennis club was very popular. So much so, that when we had to play a return match away, their Team would request that we still met at our own courts on the farm, instead of visiting them, to which no objections were raised. The attraction was the fact they could bring the children with them. Rita and Daphne entertained them so well we had little contact with them all day. Daphne gave them frequent rides on her horse "Rex" and they had the cubby house to play in.

When tennis was finished we would have another snack meal, then sago was sprinkled liberally along the wide front verandah to make it slippery and we would dance to the music of the Gramaphone, operated by Rita. Tunes such as "The Desert Song", "The Pagan Love Song", "Whispering", "Happy Days are Here Again" and many other old favourites were played. Ted and some of the men retired to the living-room for a game of cards, usually "Nap" or "Five Hundred".

The two or three small children went to sleep on the side verandah beds. Old Jim Holden was in his element, constantly making pots of tea. There was never any alcohol and it made a very pleasant ending to an enjoyable day. The visiting teams always catered for all meals when it was their turn.

Our tennis club

1933

Grandma Sunderland had been failing in health for some months. She was now 89 years of age. She had always been a strong healthy person and never needed any medical attention even though she had had 18 children - Ted being the 17th. When 87 years, old she still carried kerosene buckets of milk and grain to feed the pigs and would rake up the chips around the big wood heap, often in the moon-light. She was then quite prepared to let Jim feed the pigs but still remained active with the rake and burning off the little piles of chips. Gradually she had to relinquish this too.

Our neighbour, Annie Robinson (who was also Ted's cousin) came over to see her when she heard Grandma had been in bed for a few days and was getting weaker. Annie quickly realised the end was near and took matters in hand very efficiently. She asked me to go to Dubbo and buy material to make a shroud, such was the custom in those days, as she thought it best Ted should remain on the farm. I drove the T-model Ford Utility into town and purchased the necessary items. By the time I returned home, Grandma had passed peacefully away. She was subsequently laid to rest in the churchyard of the little Rawsonville Anglican Church of St James. Grandma's death on January 19th was an especially sad day for Rita, her 12th Birthday.

During the summer months, we often went to Clarrie Taylor's open air Picture Show. It was situated in Victoria Park almost opposite the Monarch Picture Palace and

Charlie Enderry's Cafe. We sat in canvas deck chairs and never missed seeing a Jeanette McDonald - Nelson Eddy film.

Ice cream vendors were kept busy, especially on a warm night. At other times we would drive over and pick up the Robinson family as there was plenty of room on the back of the "International" and then travel to Narromine for cold drinks and ice cream.

With regard to the affairs of the Estate, they were now causing us considerable concern. The death of Grandma meant everything related to estate matters had to be finalised.

In his Will, Ted's father had appointed two executors, his son Fred and Mr J T Steel who was the Dubbo Bailiff. Both men were now deceased and accordingly it became the obligation of Mrs Steel, the widow, to appoint another Executor. She named "The Public Trustee Company" and they took control. It was disastrous for us financially.

Ted was no longer a free agent, every estate transaction was transferred to them. To augment our greatly reduced income, Ted began a carrier service on his own account. During harvest he worked early and late carting wheat from neighbouring farms to the Silo at Minore Siding. Stock dealing continued with the Ganarrin Meat Company and later on he carried bales of wool, hay and lucerne when in season.

On one occasion a huge water tank was transported from

Bales of lucerne, stacked by Ted on new International *with Tom Bowness and Herb Warren*

Dubbo to Balladoran. The tank was so wide, Ted and two off-siders had to remove the railings over creek crossings to enable them to drive the lorry over.

1934

Some months ago because there had been no religious education at the little bush school for either of our girls, who were old enough to understand Bible teaching, we thought it essential they should receive some instruction. Being a Christadelphian, I decided to contact our nearest Meeting and its Recording brother. From my monthly magazine "The Christadelphian" I found it to be at Doonside, an outer suburb of Sydney, and the Recorder, Brother G. Darke. I wrote to him and explained the situation and asked if we could establish some kind of postal correspondence Sunday School tuition. Brother A. Forsdike was the S. S. Superintendent and he replied to my letter enclosing literature and questions for young students.

In January, I received an invitation from Sister Ella Forsdike for us to bring the girls and spend a weekend with them so that we could all become better acquainted. Ted was unable to accompany us and I took the girls to Doonside by train. This visit began the friendship between Rita and the girls she met during our short stay, around her own age. One of them corresponded with Rita until she left school. (Her name was Gladys Reason).

We had a very bad mouse plague through the Central West of New South Wales. The mice were everywhere, literally thousands of them. They chewed clothes, shoes, books, papers, stores in the cupboards and anything in a packet or carton.

We kept our bread in a large milk churn with a tight metal lid, our meat in a hanging safe and everything else that was edible we packed in the large cool safe on the side verandah. Ted had built this safe two or three summers ago. It was quite a large construction - a strong wooden frame six feet high, four feet wide, with four deep shelves inside. Hessian covered the back and s ides, also the wide door in the front. The whole unit stood in a six inches deep galvanised tray of water. On top was a similar tray full of water. Immersed in this were long strips of blanket - one end in the water, the other hanging down the hessian back and sides, dripping moisture continuously. With air along the verandah on the wet cover, the safe was always cool. The butter did not melt on the hottest day - it was absolute protection from ants, flies and especially mice. The hay stacks were ruined. They were alive with mice eating the heads of grain.

The plague lasted several weeks and then a disease of some kind developed in the swarms of them and they vanished, fortunately not leaving too many behind to be quickly cremated in the big clean-up . Everything in the house had to be scrubbed with Lifebuoy sand soap, a strong disinfectant - all the furniture, cupboards, shelves and floors. Eventually it was done.

Dickygundi School

Daphne off to school
on Hazel, my pony

1935

We did not possess a motor-car. Our vehicles were the big International lorry and the T-Model Ford Utility. There was always produce to be taken to Dubbo and stores and shopping to bring back and deliver.

Early in the year (February 6th) Ted had some business to transact in Sydney and decided to drive down for a few days. We borrowed Arthur Sunderland's "Dodge" Car - an open tourer and he took the utility to use in our absence. Ted and I set off on a terribly hot day. The car at the best of times was not in good shape. In the high temper-ature, the water in the radiator constantly boiled. We had to stop several times and let it cool down. One memorable stop was when we reached Cox's River in the Blue Mountains locality. There was no fence or barrier of any kind over the crossing, so I climbed the rocky bank, found a convenient spot, sat down and removed my shoes and stockings. The water was crystal clear, almost cold and so refreshing to drink and bliss to my hot feet, as the stream tumbled down over the boulders. We managed to get half way up the Victoria Pass before it was necessary to call the next halt. We joined the queue of three or four cars in the same predicament. By this time the afternoon was well advanced and the temperature began to drop.

We were able to continue to the city where we left the car (thankfully) thankfully at a sizeable garage. The repairs would take at least a week.

Of course we had to visit the Sydney Cricket Ground to watch a Sheffield Shield match against Queensland. It was another extremely hot day as we sat on the Hill just below the score board and absolutely cooked. I bought a newspaper and spread it over my arms and legs. Fortunately in those days, large shady hats were worn, so that was a help.

Our garage account for car repairs was much higher than our Hotel bill. We had no problems on the return journey.

Ted was kept busy with his carrying business. Bert was doing very well in the market garden. We now had a small Howard rotary hoe to do much of the work in half

Paddling in a mountain stream,
clear ice cold water. It was beautiful.
I had to wade in to get a drink.
Cox's River, N.S.W. 6 February, 1935.

the time. We had a huge crop of large white onions. These were sent to the Sydney vegetable market for sale. Previous transactions had always been very satisfactory but on this occasion we were definitely defrauded. The agents sent us a cheque for two pounds, stating the rest of the consignment had sweated in transit. There was no way to prove this had been the case but it was most unlikely.

In August, Miss Nancy Bird (the aviatrix) visited Dubbo in her small plane for a week of "barnstorming" - the price was one pound (twenty shillings) per person. Ted was very keen to take a flight and asked me to go up with him. I was so fearful of flying in those early days of aviation, I refused emphatically and nothing more was said. Ted never confessed to me but I always suspected he had taken a flight with Miss Nancy Bird over Dubbo and environs. He was so enthusiastic about her achievements that it occurred to me (many months later) that it was more than likely he, too, had been a passenger while she was in Dubbo. I never queried it!!

"Back to Dubbo Week" was celebrated the first week in December, opening with a grand parade and procession with decorated floats representing various local organisations. Daphne marched with the school children in the Red Cross section.

Back to Dubbo Week, 5th December, 1935

1936

Rita finished her education at the Dubbo High School. She was very good at drawing and sketching and favoured the idea of Commercial Art. It was difficult to find someone in Dubbo to instruct her. I enquired of our mailman and he informed me his wife had been a Ticket Writer and may be able to help. Rita had a few lessons with Mrs Henderson but it was limited tuition.

Meanwhile correspondence from Doonside still urged Rita to join them with Mrs Forsdike offering accommodation. We knew Rita would be well looked after and as she was so keen to go, we consented. The local school had been closed so I applied to the Sydney Correspondence School for Daphne to receive lessons through the post. I had to supervise them and give personal attention where necessary.

Rawsonville Cricket Club organised a Spring Flannel Dance in November. Ted was the Hon. Secretary and made all the arrangements. The men wore their cream cricket flannels and the ladies attended in white tennis outfits; everybody was in light clothing. When the "New Regent Band" arrived their members had entered into the spirit of the occasion, all dressed in cream shirts and slacks as well. The added attraction was Stan Cross. He was the most popular singer in the district and sang the Perry Como type of songs.

The announcement was most surprising because a few

RAWSONVILLE CRICKET CLUB 27

SPRING FLANNEL DANCE

In the MEMORIAL HALL
Wednesday Night, November 4, 1936

NEW REGENT ORCHESTRA

Real Rawsonville Night   ::   **Special Supper**

2/5   TED SUNDERLAND, Hon. Sec.

weeks earlier he had been engaged for the season at a Katoomba Hotel to the dismay of all his fans. Ted made contact with Stan and the Hotel gave their permission for him to appear at Rawsonville. Ted also paid all his expenses. There was a "Free" bus from Dubbo (personally financed by Ted) and the dance was a great success, a truly well patronised, delightful affair.

1937

Mr Cutts, farmer and grazier of "The Camp" in the Coalbaggie district, asked Ted if he would care-take his house and property for two weeks while he took his family on holiday. I think it pleased Ted that he had been asked to do this and he willingly agreed. I still did the cooking for the share-farmers and the gardeners, so Ted took Daphne with him for company. Rita had returned to Doonside and was staying with Bev and Harry Stowe.

Caretaking at The Camp *property, 1937*

Sad to relate Grandfather Bowen passed away. A friend of Grandma Bowen, Alice Best, had also recently been widowed. She had one little boy (Peter) to support and she decided to go to Sydney and find work. She asked Grandma to go with her as the Bowen girls, Violet, Flo and Rita, were all married and Grandma was alone. Accordingly Gran sold up and left Dubbo with Alice and Peter.

Rita came home for Christmas. She was able to do some shopping for me which I had selected from Anthony Horden's Mail Order Catalogue. A coat, a large suitcase and the table board game of Halma (similar to Chinese Checkers).

Ted with a carpet snake

1938

Rita returned to Doonside after a short time. She stayed with the Darke family and obtained a job as cashier with Smith Sons & Rees in Wentworth Avenue, under Mr Charles French.

On the farm it was very hot and dry, causing another drought to set in. Daphne was now eleven years of age and a great help to her father and Mr Stan Wilkins of "Dulla Dulla". He would ring up and ask if "Dap Dap", as he always called her, (it had been "Snow" when she was little and had fair hair) would meet him at the Coalbaggie Crossing and help him move his sheep across in the right direction. As the drought continued, our stock had to be hand fed. Daphne was able to drive the big lorry in low-low gear slowly across the paddock while Ted forked hay or lucerne from the back.

Rawsonville School had been re-opened, as more children were in the district. Jack Mason was the School Teacher and rode his motor-cycle (Harley Davidson) out from Dubbo every day. In those days Jack lived at the Commercial Hotel in Brisbane Street.

Daphne's pony "Rex" had died during the drought from taking in too much sandy soil while nibbling at stunted growth in the paddock. Daphne used to walk to the end of the lane where Jack would pick her up and proceed to school on the back of the motor-bike for the remaining two miles.

The Public Trustee Company had at last finalised the affairs of the Estate of the late Thomas Sunderland, taking almost seven years to do so. The end result was disastrous. We had to sell some of our land to meet the last payments. We sold the Front Paddock of 120 acres to Jim Hopkins.

There was also another problem. This was Daphne's last year in Primary School and she would have to go on to High School in Dubbo. Now that Grandma Bowen had moved to Sydney there was no-one else to accommodate Daphne for the school week. Boarding school was the next consideration and after scouting around we decided on "Osborne Ladies College" at Blackheath in the Blue Mountains. I wrote to the Principal of the college and in reply was notified that our application had been successful.

Our share-farmers, Lock and George Robinson did not renew an agreement for 1939. Lock had purchased a small property, with cottage, on the Narromine Road adjoining Arthur Warren. George married Jack Cross's daughter Thelma and had taken over "Glen Isla" next to us where Bill and Ann Robinson had lived so long. "Glen Islaî belonged to Bill's father, old George Robinson, proprietor of the roadside Dickygundi Hotel. Bill was in temporary retirement and had moved into Mary Street, Dubbo.

Changes all around and within. It started me thinking very seriously. Our friends scattered - Rita in Sydney, Daphne soon in Blackheath, leaving Ted and myself alone on a property that would take years of hard work to recover from the long spell of mismanagement and the crippling prolonged drought.

The market garden was still successful with Bert Bracegirdle was continuing in charge. We had a few sheep, cows and horses. Our main income was derived from Ted's carrier business with the Ganarrin Meat Co and the local farmers. To abandon the carrying and concentrate on the farm did not appeal (it was one or the other).

The extended heat wave was affecting me very badly. The temperature reached 110 degrees or more during the day and did not drop below 100 degrees throughout the night. The heat from the iron roof was almost unbearable - even the water from the hose was quite warm. I went to Dr. Roper for help and he advised Ted to take me away to a cooler place where I could revive from the heat exhaustion I was suffering.

I had been toying with ideas concerning our future for several weeks. Dr. Roper's advice and opinion made up my mind and now was the time to discuss those ideas with Ted. I must admit I did so with feelings of trepidation and some reluctance. After all, "Pine Farm" was his inheritance. He was born on the property and I was about to ask him to make a momentous decision regarding it. I asked Ted if he would consider selling "Pine Farm" and moving to Sydney. We could have Rita back with us, Daphne would not have to go away to Boarding School and we would be a united family again, living in a cooler climate.

For survival we would buy a small mixed business - a shop with dwelling. I urged him to say nothing at that juncture but give the matter plenty of thought and make his own decision. On the other hand, he may think of another alternative for our future.

Christmas was uneventful. Bert from the garden joined us but there was nothing specific to record.

1939

The first week in January Ted told me, with a smile on his face that he had a buyer for "Pine Farm". To date there had been no reference to my proposal. Instead Ted had wanted to surprise me. It was a great relief to me (judging from Ted's approach) that there would be no repercussions and no emotional regret. Ted had agreed to sell the property to Mr Joe Gibbs of "Iona" and a very quick transaction and payment followed.

Ted and I went off to Sydney to buy the small business. We contacted an agency and after four days found what we were looking for at 36 King Street, Mascot (Later changed to Eastlakes). We then shopped for furniture for the dwelling. The furniture at "Pine Farm" was not worth removing to the city.

In hindsight, it was antique - Australian made cedar furniture, but I was sick of it! It would be quite valuable today.

We returned to Dubbo to pack up, go round our friends to say goodbye, attend a surprise farewell function organised by our Rawsonville friends at Enderby's Cafe in Darling Street, then load up the International lorry with our goods and chattels. We had George Robinson and Stan Wilkins to see us off from the farm. Our old Irishman had gone to work for Jim Cross. Bert had an agreement to continue with the market garden and would occupy the house.

A final wave and it was farewell "Pine Farm". My twenty years in the bush were over - February 23rd, 1919 to January 29th, 1939.

Sydney - January 1939

We arrived safely and in good time. Our new furniture had been delivered. Tom Ward, the previous owner of the business, had supervised it. He was staying for another two weeks to help us in the shop, to introduce the regular customers and commercial travellers and gave us all kinds of advice in conducting our new venture.

In those days, removable shutters had to be put in place to cover all grocery stock, cigarettes and tobacco every evening at 6.00 o'clock and Sundays during Church hours. (You could be fined if shutters were not in place. Inspectors called at any time - day or night). From memory I recall items like:- butter costing 10½d. per lb; milk 3½d. a pint - bulk milk sold by measure only; bread 5½d. a loaf and 3d. a half loaf. Cigarettes were 6d. a packet of 10. The only washing powder was "Persil"

(Rinso followed years later). Coca-Cola was launched in Sydney and we were given a case to try before placing an order, 3d. a bottle was the retail price. Deliveries were made by uniformed men in Red trucks. We did not sell newspapers but they cost 1d. each.

Rita came home to us and worked full time in the shop. She was a great help. The premises were owned by Mrs. Fielder, who lived next door with her husband and only son - Frank, a young man 22 years of age.

Mr. Ward recommended a reliable Business Insurance Company for us to contact and they sent Mr. Don Crofts, one of their representatives, to carry out all the usual procedures. He called on us frequently over a relatively short period, although it was long enough for Ted and Don Crofts to become firm friends.

Our shop, 36 King Street, Mascot, 1939

In Don's free time he taught Ted to play golf at the Brighton Golf Club. This was good for there were not enough things for Ted to do about the place to keep him fully occupied. Don continued his visits and admitted his interest in Rita.

However, Rita had made it very clear the interest was not mutual. So ended any romance with Don but we still kept in touch until 1963.

Frank Fielder and Rita began going out together in May. By the end of August they were engaged to be married. Frank owned a block of ground just down the street (number 46) and plans for building their home began in earnest. Mr Milledge next door to them, a great friend of the Fielder family, was also a builder. He accepted the contract to build their home at a later date.

Jack Milledge, their son, was a keen musician and played several instruments. Daphne wanted to learn to play the piano-accordion and under Jack's tuition became an accomplished performer.

During August, Daphne became a victim of a prevailing influenza epidemic. She was very sick. We had not yet registered with a local doctor and every surgery I called informed me the doctor was already fully booked out with so much illness around. In desperation I took Daphne's temperature (now 104 degrees), wrapped the thermometer in a hand towel and went to Dr. Darragh's surgery (recommended by Mrs. Fielder). I explained the situation and asked Dr. Darragh to read the thermometer.

He did so and without any hesitation made arrangements for his new patient to be admitted to Prince Henry Hospital at the coast. Her illness was Double Pneumonia. An eminent physician Sir Charles Bickerton-Blackburn, was attending the hospital at the time of her admission. A new drug for pneumonia, the "M and B" tablet, had just become available and Daphne was the first patient to receive it under the personal supervision of Sir Charles. It was a close call for a few days and a very anxious time for us.

Fortunately we could visit her at any hour of the day. The Rev. Horner was wonderful. He was the Congregational Minister of Mascot and the little Church two doors away from our shop. He visited her last thing every night and came to us with the latest report on her condition as there was no phone at the shop. Mercifully, she survived the crisis and slowly recovered. Our prayers had been answered.

The aggressive state of the European countries and the German Invasion of Poland one the 1st of September, 1939, culminated in the Declaration of War on the 3rd September, 1939, by Britain and the Dominions - World War II.

The Recruiting Centres for enlistment in the Services were crowded - city and country alike. In the second week of October an official O.H.M.S. letter arrived for Ted. I had a queer premonition as he read the contents. This was fully confirmed when he very self-consciously handed the notice to me. It stated: "N68708 Sergeant Edward Henry

Sunderland, 11th Garrison Battalion proceed to
Headquarters at Sydney Showground, 16th October 1939."
At first I was naturally upset and disturbed.

Ted told me that he had recently met two very old friends
from World War I, Colonel Allen Smith and Major Lloyd.
They had remained in the Army and gained promotion.
He had lunch with them and accompanied them to their
quarters to have a look around Victoria Barracks again,
having once been quartered there too.

Rev. & Mrs. S. S. W. Horner
Congregational Church, Mascot, 1939

Sgt. E. Sunderland
11th Garrison Battalion, 1940

No doubt the familiar surroundings bustling with activity and a little influence from the officers resulted inevitably in un-premeditated enlistment.

I feel it is important to state at this point, that unless a person has been closely involved with a member of the armed forces, no matter whether ex-serviceman or current Army, it is impossible for anyone else to comprehend the depth of loyalty and comradeship which exists between men-serviceman or current Army, it is impossible for anyone else to comprehend the depth of loyalty and comradeship which exists between men who have been on Active Service together. Time does not diminish the strength of this bond.

It was the first time it had affected me personally and I found it hard to accept. I was not angry and certainly not patriotic after the initial shock had subsided. I remember my reaction and my sarcastic comment to Ted, for I said to him: "If you prefer to sleep in a horse stall at the Showground instead of your own comfortable bed at home - go to it!" At this jibe, Ted was only amused and laughed heartily.

We settled down again with another change approaching. Frank and Rita had decided to be married on the 10th November at the little Congregational Church next door but one to the shop. As there was no man in the house it was a good arrangement for them to live with me until their own home was built. It was a quiet wedding and a small family reception at home.

Our good friend and neighbour, Mrs. Rose Sonter, was a great help. She supervised the wedding breakfast for me and all went well. Ted managed to get leave for the occasion and performed his duty as Father of the Bride.

1940-1949

On 25th July 1940, Rita and Frank moved into their own home at 46 King Street, Mascot (where they still reside). Rita still helped in the shop but her time was now limited and Daphne and I were left alone in the shop premises.

We carried on for a few more months and during that time I became extremely nervous. There had been so many robberies in small shops in all local suburbs (including ours) and I was afraid of the same thing happening to us. The cost of tobacco and cigarettes had increased, while at the same time were in short supply. These items were the main object of theft. I needed little persuasion from Ted to put the business up or sale. This accomplished, Daphne and I moved to a small flat in Woollahra. It was not very convenient but it served its purpose for a time until we found something more suitable. Accommodation was hard to find. Eventually we secured a self-contained unit in the next street, on the first floor of a large house which had been converted into eight flats.

By this time Daphne was able to entertain with her accordion at various functions. On two occasions she played at the Tivoli Theatre, Castlereagh Street, Sydney (now demolished) on the "Harry Yates Variety Show", entertaining members of the Armed Forces.

Our flat was ideal during summer weather but was freezingly cold in the winter; no sun penetrated into any room.

As the winter of 1942 approached, I did not feel inclined to endure another cold season there. I mentioned this to the caretaker of the flats. She quickly offered me the greater part of her much larger and sunny flat. With accommodation still hard to find, I accepted. As we only had to move from one side to the front of the building, Ted said he would get special leave and bring one of his men with him to help carry the furniture around. Outside our flat was a flight of wooden stairs with a single hand-rail, which passed by our kitchen window up to the back verandah of our new quarters (for the use of Tradesmen and milk delivery).

Ted and Ernest had practically finished the job except for my Bluebird Sewing Machine (from Pine Farm). Ted suggested he stand on the stairs outside the window and Ernest haul the machine through it to him. There were only three steps to the verandah. No problem - both men were big and strong. Ted took the machine quite firmly and leaned against the wooden hand-rail to enable him to turn to go up the three steps when the railing broke away from its post.

Ted fell heavily to the concrete yard below, landing on his knees. I had no doctor to call and while the caretaker and Ernest stayed with Ted, I rushed the short distance to Oxford Street, got on a tram to Victoria Barracks and reported the accident to a Medical Officer. I stressed the urgency and was assured of immediate action. I returned home just in time to see the Ambulance disappear, taking him to the 113th A G Hospital at Concord. It was a week before the swelling permitted operating on both broken knees. It was a miracle the accident had not been fatal. The sewing machine bumped down the stairs to the yard. Later I had it repaired.

It was nine months before Ted was able to return to Military duty and many weeks passed before he was capable to travel home on sick leave.

During this period, on May 31st, 1942, two Japanese midget submarines entered and attacked shipping in Sydney Harbour, killing nineteen naval ratings at night. The alarm sirens sounded throughout the city area. The caretaker of our building assembled all the tenants in the largest ground floor flat. We were all in night attire, dressing gowns and slippers and I must admit a little apprehensive. All except an elderly lady, the occupier of the flat, who was sitting in an arm-chair quite composed and dignified - fully dressed, complete with her handbag and wearing a hat. We remained there until the "All Clear" siren sounded.

Ted told me later of all the activity at the Concord Military Hospital immediately the Alarm had been sounded. All the patients who could be moved were laid on mattresses on the floor under their beds while arrangements were rapidly made with a fleet of ambulances to transfer them to the Kenmore Hospital at Goulbourn. I was duly notified of the transfer and letters were the only contact we had with Ted for a long period.

I did not have sufficient things to do to fully occupy my time so decided to get a job. I found an interesting advertisement in the paper for a person wanted to read to an elderly lady who lived in Bellevue Hill (within walking distance). I went to the given address, knocked on the door and was greeted by a man servant who looked as sinister as "Lurch", the butler in the Addam's Family TV show. I stated my business and without saying a word he beckoned me to follow him down a long corridor into a room where a white-haired old lady sat stiffly upright in a wooden chair. She asked me a few personal questions then handed me *The Sydney Morning Herald* and told me to read the whole of the front page to her.

She was quite satisfied and said so without any sign of relaxing her stern attitude. Next she asked me which Political Party I voted for. I told her I belonged to the Christadelphian Faith and was exempt from voting, on the grounds of our religious beliefs. She suddenly became very antagonistic and in a loud voice accused me of being all sorts of things - such as disloyal, ungrateful, irresponsible, and a parasite. On hearing the raised angry voice the faithful "Lurch" came hastily to the room to investigate. I immediately demanded that he escort me to the front door and with great relief I left the premises.

My next venture was to apply to the General Post Office in Martin Place, Sydney, for the position of Mail Sorting Officer currently being advertised. The interview was brief. On my application I stated the period I had conducted the Rawsonville Sub-Post Office on "Pine Farm" which influenced my successful appointment. There was quite a number of other young women engaged at the same time owing to the vacancies caused by the mail sorters enlisting in the Services. On our first day the new staff were given a conducted tour over the entire building, finishing in the basement presently equipped as the Air Raid Shelter for all the employees in case of an Alert Warning.

There was a great deal to learn in the Sorting Department and much to memorise. I enjoyed the work, intense though the concentration had to be. In those days post codes had not been thought of. You had to know the postal areas and the towns included therein, decipher the destination of each letter and sort into relevant pigeon holes. Unfortunately I had only been employed there a few weeks when a health problem developed which left no alternative to me but to resign. I abandoned the idea of a job.

Ted was making good progress and was allowed home, on crutches, for Christmas. He would not be able to resume military duties again and eventually was discharged from the Army on April 22nd, 1943, when he was able to dispense with support for his legs. I received short notice of the impending discharge and immediately endeavoured to find some suitable house or ground floor flat before Ted arrived. The flat Daphne and I shared was not at all convenient under the circumstances. Accommodation was still hard to find in an acceptable area and I drew blanks everywhere.

One of the offices gave me a telephone number of a city agency. I rang and in reply was told the only vacant property they had listed was an empty shop with

dwelling at Summer Hill. Daphne and I set off post haste
to an address I had been given in that suburb, to obtain
the key. A bit daunting when we got there - it was in the
centre of a little row of shops. The shop window was
completely boarded up to comply with Air Raid
regulation. However, we went in and made our inspection of the premises. The shop had been stripped of all
fittings and shelves. It was just a big empty room.
Behind it was the staircase, then the kitchen, living room,
laundry and toilet. The back door opened on to a
pocket-handkerchief lawn with back entrance to a lane.
Upstairs were three bedrooms and a bathroom with a
very old fashioned chip heater. It was quite efficient
although it terrified me.

Once the light wood was ignited the whole contraption
rocked and roared with flames crackling in the container.
One redeeming feature was the sufficient near boiling hot
water was available in a few minutes. The entire place
was remarkably clean.

The agency was about to close as it was late afternoon
when I had phoned, so I could not contact them until the
following morning. They found me waiting for them to
open. In a short while I was signed up for tenancy of
119 Smith Street, Summer Hill.

It was great to have Ted permanently home with us again
and I was glad his military service had definitely ended.
He had been instructed to register for employment at the
Ashfield Government Labour Exchange. Whatever job
was offered had to be accepted under war-time man-

power regulations. To our dismay Ted was sent to
"Malleable Castings" foundry at Newtown - a terrible job -
in May 1943. He had to remove a full container of hot
liquid metal suspended from a revolving 'endless chain'
and replace it with an empty one. I must admit he did
not complain. During 1944, while working in this manner, an accident occurred. Hot metal from the next container was mishandled by the man in charge standing
next to Ted and some of the liquid splashed on Ted's legs
and sprayed hot floor sand inside his boots.

He was treated immediately by the company doctor and
nurse employed on the premises. The burns were not
large but numerous and he was sent home with
instructions to return daily for dressings. This treatment
continued for weeks with reduced income on
compensation. The legs did not heal and resulted in the
development of varicose eczema and Ted had to wear an
elastic stocking on each leg.

On the 1st September, 1944, our first grandchild was
born. Rita and Frank's first baby Edward Charles Fielder.
Ted was quite sure his new grandson would eventually
become a cricketer and he bought a junior cricket set and
had the stumps erected on the back lawn of their home
the day Rita brought the little fellow home.

In the meantime Daphne and Roger Wigmore, a
young member of our Christadelphian Meeting, had
become special friends and often spent weekends with
his parents at "The Bobbin Inn" Bobbin Head Resort.
Christmas 1944 approached and Roger was staying with

us.

During the week previous to the holiday, it was announced on the radio that three British Warships would be in Sydney Harbour and it was suggested that people in private homes could extend hospitality to the servicemen aboard these ships for the festive period. Ted immediately asked me if I would like to do so - of course he knew I would. Instruction was given to call at an office in Queen's Square and leave name and address and a couple of navy personnel would be directed to our address. It was already the weekend and Christmas Day was Monday.

Ted and I, Roger and Daphne all attended our Christadelphian morning service on Christmas Eve, after which Roger and Daphne returned to Summer Hill to finish the decorations and prepare a roast dinner for our expected guests.

Ted and I found the office but it was closed. We decided to have lunch and talk the situation over. Ted came up with the idea of looking for two British Marines whose appearance appealed to me and who might be happy to accept our invitation. We walked along to St James Station and sat on a seat at the edge of Hyde Park. There were men in uniform everywhere. I indicated two young Petty Officers for Ted to approach. They were a little hesitant at first then said they would have to return to their ship first but would meet us here again at four o'clock. It was a long wait and they did not return. I was so disappointed I opted to go home. Ted suggested cheerfully I might spot two likely looking lads on our way to the Town Hall Station. We did not see any until we reached Bebarfald's Corner, outside the station entrance. I saw these two boys and quickly nudged Ted. One lad was very tall - his mate much shorter.

Ted asked them if they would like to come and share Christmas with us and two other young people in our home. The tall boy responded eagerly, with a beaming smile "Can we come now?" We introduced ourselves and met:- Musician P R McAlister and Musician A L Dawkins, Royal Marine Band, H.M.S. "HOWE" and proceeded to Summer Hill in a gay mood. On arrival, just before 6.00pm, Roger and Daphne welcomed Peter and Les and were curious to know why we had been such a long time. After explanations, the visitors helped with the last of the decorating streamers. Peter's height was a big advantage. Roger supervised a lovely dinner (he was an excellent chef) and we all enjoyed the meal.

I must record right here, that on this particular day (24th December, 1944), Peter McAlister entered our home and our family and through all the years since, he and his lovely family have always remained in close contact and affection with all of us. I call him my adopted son, because that is the way I regard him. I am sure the regard is reciprocated.

After our visitors had retired for the night, we decided we would have a bit of fun with them and maintain the Christmas spirit. It was Christmas Eve. Accordingly we filled two stockings with fruit and nuts at the foot, a couple of handkerchiefs, Christmas trivia and lollies etc., labelled them and hung them on the door handle outside their room.

The boys enjoyed "Santa's" visit Christmas morning and after an early breakfast had to report back to their ship. To our great amusement Peter and Les set off to the railway station each with his tinsel decorated stocking hung over his shoulder.

They returned later that day. Their stay was short as they soon set sail for an undisclosed destination. Peter kept in touch with us writing several letters and saying how much he looked forward to a return visit to Sydney.

1945

On New Year's Day, Roger and Daphne, Ted and myself all attended the early morning meeting at the Christadelphian Hall in Regent Street, after which we planned to go and watch a Sheffield Shield cricket match at the Sydney Cricket Ground.

The tram terminus was only a short distance from the Hall and trams were running direct to the S.C.G. Bro. Tom Drinkwater was waiting at the stop for the same tram so he joined us. During the lunch break Ted excused himself to go and see if he could find Mr Wally Gorman, the curator of the Ground. They had become good friends while Ted was in the Army and stationed at the S.C.G.

Ted returned to us after some time only to say Mr. Gorman was short of staff and had asked him to take charge of the Ticket Stile as people were still arriving for the afternoon play. By the end of the day Mr. Gorman had asked Ted to change his job and work at the cricket ground, operating the Ticket stile for every match played there. This offer was accepted with enthusiasm. Ted had to notify the Labour Exchange that he would be leaving the Foundry immediately and starting his new occupation at the end of the week.

Meanwhile, Daphne and Roger became engaged and set the 25th August for their wedding date.

One day early in the year, we had a surprise visitor. I answered the ring of the door bell and a young British Marine greeted me with a broad smile and said "I am Michael McAlister, Peter's brother. He gave me your address and told me to call and see you". We made him very welcome and he spent his entire leave with us, quite happy to relax and listen to music on the Radio. We also had a similar visitor a short time later. He introduced himself as Fred Dawkins, younger brother of Les and he came to us for all his leave too. Both Michael and Fred paid us several visits and sometimes brought their mates. By the end of the War our "Marine boys" must have numbered nine or ten guests in all. There had only been one condition - no alcohol and this was observed.

Peter always spent his leave with us and he would tell me of the girls he met. After a close description and the answers to a few queries, I would express my opinion.

Then it happened - Peter had discovered a super girl at the Catholic Recreation Club for Servicemen and he definitely wanted us to meet her. I was favourably impressed and suggested peter bring her for tea on Sunday. Late on Saturday afternoon, I washed my hair and left it set in curlers to dry. Ted made a special request to have bacon and eggs for our evening meal. This we did and before I could clear the table afterwards, the door bell rang. It was Peter and his new girlfriend. So we met Miss Aileen Kernahan for the first time.

I felt terribly self-conscious, my hair in curlers, a pinafore over my dress and the place reeking with the smell of recently cooked bacon. It didn't seem to matter as the atmosphere was so congenial. Peter's excuse was that he couldn't wait another day to bring Aileen out to "Mum and Popî. Before they left, Aileen assured me they would still attend the Sunday invitation (next day).
My advice to Peter of complete approval is all past history and so Aileen joined the Sunderland circle as one of the "family".

I enjoyed that summer of 1945 as I often accompanied Ted to the Cricket Ground and watched the game from a privileged seat in the Ladies Stand while Ted was on duty. World War II ended in Europe in May but was not over between America and Russia against Japan. The first Atom Bomb fell on Hiroshima on August 6th and another one on Nagasaki on August 9th. Hirohito signed formal surrender on September 2nd.

Rationing had been established during the war and

coupons were necessary to obtain many items, such as food and soft goods etc. The number of coupons per person was limited and we needed more for wedding dresses. Daphne's friends were very helpful and gave her all their spare coupons so she was able to buy sufficient material for the event. Daphne and Roger were married at the Christadelphian Hall, Regent Street, August 25th, 1945. The Reception was held at Amory, Ashfield.

1946

The highlight of 1946 was the holiday Ted and I spent for two weeks at the "Prince of Wales" Hotel at Nowra, N.S.W.. Wally Watson was our genial host and made sure we enjoyed his hospitality. The weather was perfect and we spent most of the time fishing in the beautiful Shoalhaven River, way up stream. Ted hired a little motor boat to do this. A small cafe, close to the hotel, packed us a mid-day lunch with a thermos of tea at a very reasonable cost for every trip we made. The fishing was good and we shared our catch between the cafe and our hotel. We enjoyed several bus tours to beauty spots and neighbouring towns, went to the pictures or played cards at night.

Later in the year, the agent who collected our rent, asked me if I would like to live in a new brick semi-detached cottage, now being built at Enfield. He gave me the address and suggested we go and inspect the building and the location and if favourable, select which dwelling I preferred.

My delight at the prospect was very evident. Ted and I lost no time in going to Bede Street Enfield, expecting to find the semis almost complete. Instead there was little more than the foundations laid and no workmen on the job. However, we were satisfied with everything and gladly signed up with the agent and paid the first week's rent of 30 shillings for No. 9 Bede Street, with a wait of five months.

1947

Rita and Frank's second child was born on February 6th. Another son "Raymond Frank".

By the time we finally received notice to occupy the premises at Bede Street, it was June and that section of the locality had become South Strathfield. Ted had a lot to do -preparing a lawn and garden, while I organised things in the house.

I decided to hang the new kitchen curtains at the window over the sink while Ted, Daphne and Roger were at work. I removed my shoes and climbed up on the white porcelain sink. I had to screw the brackets for the curtain rod into the wall with a ratchet screwdriver. I realised I would have to change my position to gain more leverage. As I turned to do this, my stockinged feet slipped on the smooth polished surface and as I fell, I struck the back of my head on the corner of the Ice Chest and landed in the sink. I was quite unable to move for several minutes - then managed to scramble to the floor, only to find it was too painful to try and stand upright. I shuffled along to our bedroom and gradually got on the bed where I remained until the family came home and Daphne prepared a late evening meal. I expected to have some bruises as evidence of my fall but there were none. I only felt a little stiffness the next day.

1948

Daphne and Roger were expecting their first baby at about the end of March. Daphne had a very complicated pregnancy and sadly the tiny infant "Peter Roger" born on April 1st only survived a short time.

The following spring, before the cricket season commenced Ted and I went for a holiday to Coolangatta, Queensland. We spent two weeks there and stayed at the "Kirrabelle" Hotel - not five star but comfortable. We went on several bus tours to Brisbane, where we visited the famous Gabba Cricket Ground and Surfers Paradise. We all paid six-pence each to look through the newly built hotel of the same name. Maybe that was the beginning of the development of that locality into the resort it is today.

Another exciting event was the return of Peter to Australia. He was still in the British Navy but was on marriage leave. He and Aileen had planned their Wedding for 9th September. Peter spent the pre-wedding night with us at South Strathfield.

Of course we all wore new outfits for the occasion. The sensational fashion called "The New Look" had just been introduced and Daphne's dress was carried out in detail. It was a beautiful wedding. Aileen's father, Mr Vince Kernahan, invited us to join the Bridal party after the ceremony, to witness the signing of the Register as representatives for Peter's family. The Wedding Reception was held at "Miss Bishop's".

Over the New Year period, the Cricket Testimonial match was played for the benefit of Bert Oldfield (famous wicket keeper) and Alan Kippax (very fine batsman). Through Ted's employment at the S.C.G., I was asked to sit at a table inside the Member's gate and acknowledge the cheques and donations placed in a large box on the table. I had a great day meeting so many well known people and cricketers. Mr Keith Miller, the notable all-rounder, was very friendly and gave me an opportunity to produce my autograph book. He obliged willingly and offered to take my book and obtain various signatures of the players. He returned the book personally after lunch, quite elated because (Sir) Donald Bradman had given his autograph among other cricketer's of international fame. Kippax and Oldfield received six thousand pounds each.

1949

Nothing very eventful happened in the early part of the year. I thought it was unique that in January our rent collector informed me that our rent had been reduced to 27/6 from 30 shillings per week because we had made several improvements of our own volition. Ted had erected a lattice fence and gate across the side entrance path, painted the window frames and had built a lean-to shelter at the back of the house for the lawn mower and garden tools.

Ted had to work at the S.C.G. on the Queen's Birthday holiday in June. I woke early and decided I would make a cup of tea. I sat up in bed, opened my arms for a good stretch and was seized by an excruciating pain in the back of my neck.

Ted thought I had a severe cramp but I could not bear the gentle massage. Daphne heard the commotion and explanation and went next door to ask Mrs. Mills to ring for her doctor. We had not enrolled with a doctor since changing our address but Mrs. Mills assured us Dr. Frank Read from Strathfield would come immediately even though it was around 6.00am. I was still sitting up in bed, afraid to move, when he arrived a very short time later. He evidently came straight from his bed as he was wearing a pyjama coat, dark trousers, an Army sheepskin jacket and suede slippers with one big toe protruding. He was a big, tall man with an "Air Force" moustache. I observed all this while he was talking to Ted and Daphne. My pain had gradually subsided.

Dr Read examined my neck closely but did not touch me. He said I had damaged the 4th and 5th vertebrae of my spine. He said he would arrange for an X-Ray at Dr. James Burwood X-Ray Centre.

Transport was the next thing to be considered. Daphne phoned Frank and Rita, told them what had happened and Frank said he would come and take me to Burwood.

We persuaded Ted to go to work, especially as he had just been promoted from the Public Ticket stile to the Member's special gate, following the retirement of Mr. Dan French.

I was handled with the utmost care at X-Ray and a little later took the plates to Dr Read at Strathfield. After reading them, he asked me if I had had a fall recently and I assured him nothing had occurred. Then he suggested I think back over a period of time. Suddenly I remembered the bad fall which had happened exactly two years ago when we first moved to South Strathfield and I tried to put up the curtains but slipped on the sink, striking the back of my head on the ice chest.

"That's it" he exclaimed, "you damaged the cartilage between the 4th and 5th vertebrae and it has taken two years for it to decay and now your 4th and 5th are sitting on top of each other. Hospital and plaster is the next thing which I will arrangeî. Dr. Read came the next morning and took me in his car to the "Masonic" Hospital, Ashfield.

My neck up to my ears then across my shoulders and chest were padded with thick white felt. My head was tilted back and then plaster was slapped onto the felt. Dr Read and a Sister did the job but when it was finished I was quite unable to stand up due to the enormous weight of the wet plaster. I remained in hospital until the plaster had dried out and I could stand alone. Owing to the bulk and thickness of the "collar", I could not lie down in bed, so at home our two large lounge chairs were pushed together , opposite each other - I sat propped up in one, with my legs in the other. (Being a small person is sometimes an advantage). The heat from the felt padding and the irritation of my skin under it was of the utmost discomfort, without mentioning the pain! Roger was Chef at the "Monterey" Restaurant in George Street and it was usually midnight by the time he arrived home. He was never too tired to shake the pillows at my back to ease my sitting position, then he would give me my potassium bromide mixture before he retired.

I was so grateful for his care and help during that painful period.

Nearly three months later, Dr. Read removed the collar. Everyone was astonished when Ted weighed it and found its weight was 15lbs! I have only been able to turn my head halfway to left or right ever since.

1950-1959

Ted's sister Ettie, still very unfriendly towards me, now lived in Stanbrook Street, Fairfield. We had visited each other occasionally and then half way through the year, she suddenly began regular weekly visits to us and after a time we noticed she was losing weight and had swollen ankles. I suspected there was something very wrong. Ted and I discussed the change in her and decided to go and visit her.

On 12th September we paid her a visit and Ted talked to her about it. She admitted she was having medical treatment and had to go to Parramatta Hospital for tests the following week. Ted asked if she felt lonely and she said she had become very nervous and often scared at night. This was entirely out of character. We suggested she come and stay a few weeks with us until her health improved. She declined because she had no-one to look after poultry and ducks that she kept. We were so concerned about her, Ted and I decided to go to Fairfield and stay with her - whether welcome or not. It was evident she needed help. We packed our cases and landed at her door nine days after our last visit, it was now September 21st.

She was surprised to see us and told us to leave our suitcases outside on the verandah. A short time later over a cup of tea, Ted explained because of her previous disclosures we had come to stay for a while and keep her company. She was very vocal and refused to agree to any kind of reasoning, nor did she want us to remain with her. Ted appeared to submit to her protests, then remarked quite definitely that he would call and see her doctor in Fairfield on our way home and have a talk with him. Ettie knew Ted meant what he said and changed her mind very quickly. The suitcases were brought inside and we sat down again while Ettie confessed she was having fluid drained frequently from her body at her Doctor's surgery and he had organised her appointment for tests at Parramatta Hospital, where I accompanied her later.

I made shopping in Fairfield (Fairfield Heights was only a residential area in those days - one butcher and a small general goods shop) my excuse for an interview with the doctor, Dr. Rickard. He told me Ettie had cancer and it was terminal. He was very relieved to know we had come to look after Mrs Jones. She had been told she had a gland disorder and we must not enlighten her. If Ettie secretly suspected she had cancer she never gave any indication - the word was never mentioned. As a result of the hospital test she was admitted to Parramatta Hospital on October 24th for a stomach operation but the cancer was too far advanced to permit surgery. She was discharged November 8th.

The weekly fluid drainings were cancelled. Consequently the fluid in her body built up rapidly, her arms and legs swelling to such an extent she could not use her limbs to get in or out of bed without help - the weight was enormous. She was a big woman and because of the weight and swelling it was only a short time before I could no longer cope myself. We could not obtain any trained nursing aid anywhere or outside help of any description. (In those days of 1950, many people thought cancer was contagious).

Our only solution was for Ted to leave his work at the Sydney Cricket Ground where he had been employed for almost six years and stay home to help with the nursing, keep the fire going under the fuel copper and look after the poultry. The excess fluid seeped through Ettie's skin. We had to wrap towels and cloths around her and change them as they became saturated. That was the reason for the fuel copper to be kept boiling all day long and every day. We often had as many as 80 items in one day to wash and dry, using them as each batch dried on the clothes line. It saved having to change the sheets constantly.

Prior to our move to care for Ettie, Roger and Daphne had been living in a house just around the corner from us, so they were able to check on our home but as the weeks went by, with returning home an utter impossibility and rent still to be paid for the empty dwelling, Roger and Daphne moved back to our place and sold their home in Anselm Street. Daphne was also pregnant at that time.

There were no celebrations for Christmas or New Year. Ettie's condition deteriorated daily and we were in constant demand. On one of their visits to us, Roger fixed up a push button bell which Ettie kept under her pillow. It was in frequent use, especially during the night. It was a strenuous time and also a very sad one - the swelling did not abate. Very early in the morning of January 18th she rang her bell. I answered it and she wanted Ted as well. She said she knew she had not long to live and wanted to make a new will.

She asked Ted if he would live in her house permanently if she left the property to him, as this was what she wanted. It was a great surprise to us because Ettie had openly favoured another person for a considerable time, so that it entirely obliterated any conjecture as to the contents of her will.

Ted agreed to her wish and she sent me to the neighbours across the street to ask them to come over and witness the transaction. (She had always kept a blank Will form with her private papers). The neighbours obliged and left at 7.00am!

I remember taking Ettie her morning tea a little earlier than usual as breakfast had been early too. We had changed all the towel wrappings and I was amazed as I fixed her tray, to hear her tell me how much she now regretted the unkind way in which she had always treated me, especially as I was the only one, with Ted, who had come to care for her for so long. She added she had never tried to know me and was very sorry. I assured her it no longer mattered as we were now on friendly terms and could stay that way.

It was fortunate for us the fluid discharge was much less - better for Ettie and not so much washing for us. Ted had not left the house since September and a neighbour came in to cut his hair and have a chat from time to time.

1951

We had spent a very quiet Christmas and New Year and now it was 18th January 1951. The doctor called in the evening and gave Ettie an injection to settle her down for the night and just before midnight she quietly passed away.

Our next problem was for Ted to find work. He was 59 years of age and we were not very financial. However, through his cousin Pat Reid, who worked at the S.T.C. (Standard Telephone & Cables) Works at Liverpool, he was assisted in obtaining employment there.

On the 22nd April, Daphne & Roger's little son "Andrew Roger" was born. This time all went well.

Ted now had the time to do some gardening and we soon had our own vegetables. The number of ducks had also increased.

1952

It was decided later in the year that Daphne, Roger and Andrew should leave South Strathfield and live with us on the half-acre property at Fairfield.

In the meantime King George the 6th had died from cancer on 6th February and his eldest daughter, Princess Elizabeth, succeeded to the Throne. The Coronation to take place in 1952

I had received disturbing news from my brother in England concerning the health of my mother, she was not at all well. Ted too was causing us quite a lot of worry with his weight loss so apparent.

1953

Writing this book from 1897, the year of my birth, until the end of 1952, I have had to rely on the recollections from my own memory entirely. For this ensuing year, 1953, I kept a small diary which is proving a great help with dates and details.

Early in January, Ted and Daphne had a long talk about a possible trip to England. Ted was still losing weight and we were all concerned about him, including Dr. Frank Read who thought a trip would be very beneficial.
The final outcome was that Ted gave Daphne Power of Attorney to arrange finance.

On 14th January, Daphne went to the P & O Shipping Co to book our passages only to find the Line was booked out owing to the Coronation of the Queen. However, we were advised to be fully prepared with passports, taxation clearance etc., pending any cancellations.

On 29th January Daphne called at the P & O Offices just to check and to our surprise came home with two tickets for R.M.S. Chitral, due to sail on February 4th - short notice but we were ready. I must record that during these last three weeks, Daphne had bought the material and made six attractive summer frocks, sewing early and late, for my trip. She also re-shaped and trimmed one of her hats for me.

Accordingly, on February 4th we embarked at 2.00pm and R.M.S. Chitral sailed at 4.00pm in brilliant sunshine and lots of streamers.

We had a beautiful Deck Cabin, twin beds with bedside lights, a dressing table with a large mirror and H + C hand basin and there was ample space. I could sit at the window and watch the deck activities outside or just close the louvres for privacy. The "Chitral" docked 4 days at Melbourne. Ted and I spent most of the time at the

M.C.G. watching the 5th Cricket Test match, Australia v
South Africa with a crowd of 50,000 spectators. We saw
Neil Harvey make 202 runs (later records reveal this was
the top score he made in his cricket career). Australia all
out 520.

We spent our fourth day shopping and sight seeing.
Our next stop was in Outer Harbour, Adelaide, where we
went ashore for 2 days then sailed for Fremantle W.A.
During that time I developed three large mouth ulcers
and needed medical treatment. I went to the ship's
surgery and saw the surgeon. He was very pleasant with
a strong Scottish accent (Dr. D. M. Cunningham). He prescribed "Gentian Violet" and it proved effective. It took
three days from Adelaide to Fremantle.

We arrived on an extremely hot morning but went ashore
regardless. We went by bus to Perth, had a tour of the
city then shopped at "Boan's" and returned to the ship.
We sailed that evening at 6.00pm. A quarter of an hour
later the loud speaker announced Mrs. Sunderland was
wanted at the Bureau and there I received a big surprise.
A lovely bouquet of flowers from Daphne, Roger and
Andrew, their farewell gesture as we left Australia behind.
During the voyage there was plenty of entertainment. A
good Sports Committee organised games and competitions every day and after dinner at night, there would be
a dance or a card party.

We left Fremantle 16th February and on the morning of
25th February, I was awakened very early by unusual
noises which did not belong to the "Chitral" which

seemed to be scarcely moving. There was the close
splash of oars and a number of male voices, all shouting
together in a foreign language. Then I noticed the
gradual invasion of a peculiar odour - rather pungent but
not really unpleasant. It was the smell of "The East". I
looked through our cabin window and realised we were
entering the harbour of Colombo, the capital of Ceylon.
(Several years later Ceylon was changed to Sri Lanka.)
I woke Ted - it was still dark, except for the harbour
lights and he decided to stay in bed. I donned dressing
gown and slippers and went to join the other passengers
already on deck, also in robes and slippers who were
likewise eager to see what was going on with so much
activity.

As the lights disappeared in the oncoming daylight, we
were able to distinguish the names of other big passenger
liners and cargo vessels at anchor. We were moving very
slowly down a water-way with all kinds of ships on either
side. Eventually the tugs had the "Chitral" in position for
her berth.

I returned to our cabin and found our coloured Goanese
deck steward (called by the quaint name "High Finance")
had prepared my bath. The bath water, nicely treated,
was desalinated sea water and there was an overhead
shower of fresh water to rinse it off. We did not hurry
down to breakfast as so many passengers had booked for
tours around Colombo. This was our third visit to Ceylon
and we only intended to go ashore to do some shopping.
I wanted to buy a pair of open sandals to wear on deck
as the weather was so hot I needed cooler footwear.

It was necessary to go by launch to the wharf (three shillings return fare). We were met by the inevitable group of natives, the most persistent salesmen imaginable. We were surrounded with voices "Velly nice, velly cheap, you look, no have to buy". We were getting very impatient when a younger native pushed his way in to us and offered to show us "velly cheap shops". We ignored him but he made a gap for us to proceed to the piazza (veran-dah). We had no luck but every time we emerged from a shop there was the young native, in his long striped cotton shirt and long narrow skirt, waiting for us and asking us to follow him. I christened him the "Black Shadow". Being unsuccessful, we finally gave in when he assured us he knew where we could buy the sandals we told him we were looking for.

We walked a tremendous distance, in scorching heat, to a small group of shops. The Black Shadow bowed us into one of them which had a few boxes on a shelf and a long enclosed cabinet - no glass front, a table and some chairs and best of all, a very large fan rotating from the ceiling. Our black guide informed the proprietor we wanted size 4 ladies sandals and he said he would send for them while we sat and cooled down. In the meantime he set out a big tray of jewellery from the cabinet on a black velvet cloth.

It took ages to convince him we had no intention of buying any of it and to my query re sandals he snapped, No size 4" and walked away, confirming our suspicion that we had been completely fooled. The only good thing was the long cool rest out of the heat. The Black

Shadow was still waiting for us and Ted hold him to GET LOST in no uncertain manner. We learned later that natives like the "Black Shadow" were employed by a shop owner to meet tourists at the wharf and escort them to the shop as a sure way of getting customers.

We made our own way back to the main street while a very severe thunderstorm was in progress. It was frightening and there was no shelter anywhere. It proved to be a dry storm but everything, people included, were bathed in a strong, eerie copper light.

The Chitral was due to sail at 4.00pm. Shortly before that time whilst sitting on deck, I noticed a string of barges, a number of launches and other assorted craft approaching.

We moved promptly on time and that was the signal for them to surround us and follow. The tugs guiding us out of the harbour to the open sea gave a little toot and all the big liners and cargo vessels that were tied up, all sounded their sirens non-stop, the craft escorting us joining in as well. The noise was deafening but this was a ceremonial 'farewell' to the "Chitral", as it was her last voyage between England and Australia. As the tugs left us, the sirens stopped blaring and the Chitral gave one long blast in farewell.

A little later, messages sent by radio as we sailed away were pinned on the notice board:
FROM: S.S. CANNON Goodbye & good luck.
FROM: SIGNAL STATION Well done & goodbye.
FROM: H.M.S. WREN Well done thou faithful servant.

FROM: R.M.S.CHITRAL in reply, Thank you, Goodbye all.

On March 3rd we reached Aden. The British seaport at the south-west end of the Arabian peninsula before the entrance to the Red Sea. We had a rest in the cabin after dinner because we were not due to dock until 12.30am. There was some delay in passengers going ashore.

However, at 2.30am the launches arrived to take us the short distance to the wharf. It was an absolutely beautiful warm clear night and the shops were kept busy with all the groups of customers. I bought a lace stole for my mother and two embroidered blouses. One of the ladies, Mrs. Williams, bought three lovely shirts for her husband who was not travelling with her (more about this shortly). We returned to the ship at 4.00am and we sailed at 7.00am. Ted and I slept until lunchtime and woke to find the temperature was very high and extremely uncomfortable which continued through to Port Suez where we stopped for three hours. Only ships officers went ashore to comply with Canal formalities. We left at 10.00am. The change in the land on either side of the Canal since we had last seen it was amazing.

Instead of sand dunes there was a wide road which ran parallel to the bank, a hospital, two military camps and a French memorial column all spaced between large tracts of cultivation. It only took eleven hours to pass through from Suez to Port Said arriving at 11.00pm with a very definite change in the weather for it was bitterly cold. Very few people went ashore. We sailed at 7.00am the next morning, had a very rough trip with gale force winds and a heavy swell right through to Marseilles, our next port of call. The pilot and mail arrived at 10.30pm. No-one left the ship but we were able to book a motor-tour for 8.00am until 11.00am the next morning. Marseilles is a fascinating city - so much history and many beautiful buildings.

We sailed at 4.00pm down the coast of Spain and more rough weather. By the time we passed through the Straits of Gibralta, some two and a half days later, conditions had improved. Six big guns fired a farewell salute to the Chitral as we passed quite near to the fortress and proceeded up the coast of Portugal and into the Bay of Biscay which fortunately was calm and sunny. Once through that treacherous area, the final Gala Landfall dinner and dance was held, it lasted all night - a superb night to remember. In the early morning, although foggy, we sighted the coast of Devon. England at last on March 20th.

The fog became much worse that night. From 8.00pm until midnight, the siren sounded every three minutes and from then the ships bell until dawn March 21st.
The fog was so dense we could only travel at half speed, with the siren in action as we moved up the River Thames. We had expected to disembark during the afternoon. It became very doubtful when we stopped from 1.00pm until 4.00pm During that time we had a very hazy look at President Tito of Yugoslavia as his vessel passed close to us. He was leaning on the rail and waved back to us. At 6.00pm it was officially announced there would be no disembarkation until the morning. We

were anchored just off our landing stage and could see all the people waiting to welcome their friends and relatives but unable to distinguish anybody - they had to find accommodation for the night.

Our poor stewards had to rush around and make up the beds in the cabins as they had been completely stripped and we passengers had to unpack suitcases for night wear. Next morning at 9.45am - still thick fog, we were given our landing cards and shortly afterwards left the ship.

Fred and Ad, my brother and his wife, were right there to meet us. They had spent the night in a hotel nearby. Fred took us to a cafe for a cuppa before setting off in his "Austin" for Portsmouth, 70 miles away, via London and Petersfield. The family were all gathered across the road on Portsdown hill, adjacent to Fred and Ad's house. Fred had phoned them from Petersfield which was not far away. Mother was there too - she was much better than I expected but looked very frail. After lunch, my dear friend Jack Mason and his wife Ida came for the afternoon. It had been 26 years since I had been home to England. We stayed in Portsmouth for the next eight days then Fred took us with Mother to Salisbury, where we had a great welcome from my elder brother Arthur and his wife Lily and especially from my cousin Olive who had also arranged for a local press interview with our photographs taken with Mother.

We stayed in England from March 22nd until November 5th. Our visit was greatly extended as there were no earlier return bookings available due to the huge number of overseas visitors for the Coronation. We spent our time on alternate visits to Mother at Salisbury in Wiltshire and Fred & Ad at Portsmouth in Hampshire. In Salisbury we had many old friends and relatives, who entertained us and often took us to revive treasured memories of the beauty spots we had not seen for so long.

Ted, Queen and Mother (Ada Soffe), 1953

We also took mother on various country coach tours which we all enjoyed. For Ted, the Salisbury Market held every Tuesday and Saturday was a great attraction. Beside a miscellaneous assortment of merchandise, clothes, china, tools, hardware just to name a few, there was also a cattle sale every Tuesday.

My brother Fred was the authorised buyer of leather goods and all traveller's requisites for the firms of nine leather craft and trunk companies in the Southern Counties. Whenever he journeyed near Salisbury he would call and pick Ted up for the day and that was quite frequent. Our visits to Fred were of much longer duration. Mother had lived alone for so many years she preferred to have the breaks. There was considerably more activity for both of us at Portsmouth. Over the years, Fred had been promoted to General Manager of the Wyndham Hender chain of leather craft shops for which he was still the buyer. In 1950 he decided to open a shop of his own in Southsea under Ad's supervision and the help of an assistant.

Fred instructed Ted to cut out knitting bags and recorder cases in coloured plastic (imitation leather) ready for his machinist to stitch together, to be sold in his shop. Ted really enjoyed the work in Fred's large workshop at home. He was also able to attend to the lawns and garden as alternative occupation. Ad was at the shop every day until 1.00pm, so I did the cooking and chores until she came home.

Jack was very good and took us for many day trips -

Salisbury, Southampton, Bognor, London, Kew Gardens and Hampton Court to name a few. Ida did not come because of their own shoe store in Cosham. Their son Desmond had taken over as Manager from Jack and Ida did the clerical and cash section.

We had one rather extraordinary experience. Jack and Ted planned to do some fishing from Southsea Beach, taking me with them in charge of the picnic basket. Unfortunately, on that particular day, it was much to windy to fish so we went for a drive, took the ferry to Gosport then along the coast to Lee-on-Solent.
We stopped to look at the view across the water when we noticed a strange and very large craft coming in to land at the naval station a short distance away. All we could see was a big flat platform just visible above the water but as it reached shallow water and gradually emerged it was enormous, like a huge steel box.
I quickly took a snapshot and was immediately warned off by shouts and waving arms from navy personnel ashore to move away.

Jack thought it might be as well if we went a short distance away and waited a while in case we were parked in a prohibited area and there could be trouble. Nothing happened and we went home and related the event to Fred & Ad.

At 10.15pm Ad answered a knock on the front door and it was Jack accompanied by Detective Inspector Havers, in full uniform, of the Portsmouth City Police. Jack informed us the Police Officer wanted to question me as to my

Ted and Queen at Kew Gardens, London, 1953

identity and use of my camera as reported from the Naval Station that afternoon. Somehow they had taken the number of Jack's car. In trying to trace the owner they found the car had originally been bought in Winchester, Hampshire, approximately forty miles away, thus the Winchester records had to be searched and the name and address given to Portsmouth Police.

They finally located Jack only to find the person with the camera was staying in another suburb easily a mile away. It was getting late so Jack offered to act as escort to Fred's house. With Fred and Jack, both local businessmen being present, the interview did not take long to establish my identity and the reason for our excursion to Lee-on-Solent but the stern manner in which the officer conducted it was incredible. However he confiscated my camera with the unfinished film safely inside it. Three days later he returned my camera, personally, minus the film which he said had been developed and printed and I was only permitted to have copies of three snaps which had been taken in the New Forest on one of our trips. One of Ted and myself and one of me standing between two donkeys.

The Inspector told me this particular snap of me was now placed beside the photograph I had taken of the naval vessel, which he said was remarkably clear, and both photographs were now in 'British Security Records".
It had taken seven hours to trace me and my camera.
Had I been connected in any way with Foreign Agents I would have had plenty of time to dispose of the film. Incidentally, the Inspector called the vessel "Landing Craft" and I did secure his autograph and rank to prove the validity of the whole clash with Security.

While at Portsmouth we received the sad news of the death of Uncle Geoffrey Denham, my mother's youngest brother, who still lived in "Thornbury", the house next to "Sunset View", my old childhood home. We all attended the funeral and before we left the village Fred saw the owner and obtained permission for us to have a nostalgic walk around the garden and this was followed with a very kind offer to look through the house. It had scarcely changed at all.

We were a little undecided about going to London to see the Coronation celebrations and enormous procession, knowing it would be very difficult to find a place where we could see anything at all. Hundreds of people were already camping in the streets everywhere. Ted and Fred were keen to go but Ad and I had almost decided to stay at home when we had a phone call. It was Sister Daisy Handley inviting the four of us to spend the following day with them and watch the entire proceedings on their new large colour TV. That settled our problem - the four of us were only too happy to accept. (Fred only had black and white TV.)

June 2nd was a very cold day with occasional rain. Phil and Daisy welcomed us at 10.15am. We saw the Queen leave the Palace, the service and Coronation in the Abbey and the procession. The Queen and the Duke looked very elegant and regal in their coach. Queen Salote of Tonga received rousing cheers, a very imposing Lady in spectacular robes; she ignored the light rain, in her open carriage and acknowledge the crowds with a smile and wave. The viewing concluded with the Royals on the Balcony.

Later that night we went on Portsdown Hill to watch the fireworks display in Portsmouth. Home at midnight. We made many new Christadelphian friends and spent a few days at their homes. Among them was Bro. George and Sister Elsie Blake of "Fountain Court" Bramshaw, so named because of the number of fountains in the extensive grounds. It was one of England's stately homes situated in the heart of New Forest and occupied a large area. The rose garden and water garden were spectacular as was the big lake in the park. George took us sightseeing in his "Humber Imperial" car. He gave us a marvellous time. Sister Elsie was an invalid, confined to a wheel-chair with Multiple Sclerosis. She had her own private resident nurse to look after her.

On another occasion we spent a week with Bro. Eric and Sister Edna Foote in Southampton. Other highlights were a tour of the West Country with Fred and Ad. We visited Exeter, Torquay, Exmoor, Ilfracombe and Bath, The Cotswolds and the Cheddar Caves. Several months later we spent a couple of weeks touring the north of England. There were elaborate Coronation decorations everywhere we went, especially at Blackpool in Lancashire. We went to the Blackpool Tower, which is 515ft high and we went to the top, then down to the huge ballroom and listened to the recital on the organ by Reginald Dixon. Returned via Birmingham and Coventry.

On October 20th we received our luggage labels and final instructions from the P & O Shipping Company to board S.S. "Maloja" from Tilbury on November 5th at 11.30am. We had a last trip to London and visited the Motor Show at Earl's Court after the usual round of buying from leather warehouses.

Next we had to go to Salisbury and say goodbye to Mother, my brother Arthur and his wife Lily, various cousins and friends. Mother had not been too well again but I was able to see her Doctor and he assured me she was much better and he would continue to care for her. When the time came for us to leave, she kissed us and wished us a safe journey back to Australia. No tears or emotion which certainly helped the parting. That was the last time I saw her.

We only had three days left. Fred and Ad said they wanted to take us out to dinner. They had to call in at the Christadelphian Hall on the way and as it was a cold night suggested we go inside with them. To our complete astonishment the Hall now had long trestle tables on three sides complete with seating to accommodate 81 guests, members of the Ecclesia, to a three course dinner organised and financed by Bro. Phil and Sister Daisy Handley.

The last evening we spent in England, Fred and Ad gave us a farewell party, inviting twenty special friends we had made to their home at Aberdare Avenue. It was a delightful hilarious evening as we played all kinds of games and had a lot of fun. By the time supper was over there was quite a different atmosphere and many tears as friends encircled Ted and I and sang "Auld Lang Syne". After bidding us, each in tune, Godspeed on our forthcoming voyage they waved goodbye and left. Two of the men-folk had done all the washing up and the four of us sat round the fire and had a last quiet chat together before retiring to bed.

November 5th we left "Aberdare" at 7.10am. It took only a few minutes for us to connect with the busy main London Road. On the corner of the first side street was a small group of people who began waving and cheering as our car approached. Two of them were holding up a large placard "Bon Voyage' and then we could see the Handley and Ruffle families as they shouted their farewells as we passed by. They must have been up very early to be waiting there for us to drive along for of course we could not stop on the highway although Fred did slow down a fraction. The gathering was a lovely gesture made by two loving friends.

We reached London in one hour and forty minutes and had breakfast at Forte's in Finsbury, on again and as we went through Islington we ran into very foggy conditions and was held up in the heavy traffic several times as the fog thickened.

We had to be on board at 11.30am. We finally made it to Tilbury Docks at 11.15am only to find there was no ship at the wharf! Waiting passengers were informed the Maloja was delayed by fog and embarkation was now scheduled for 2.30pm. We experienced delay through dense fog when we had arrived in England nine months ago and the same happened at our departure. By the time we returned from lunch at a nearby cafe, our ship was berthed and it was time to say goodbye to our dear Fred and Ad (we had already thanked them).

We sailed at 6.20pm. To our surprise, our next door cabin neighbours were Bro. Dick and Sister Edith

Mansfield, members of our own Christadelphian Meeting in Sydney.

Life aboard was very entertaining and the weather was good. We reached Algiers on November 11th at 7.00am, went ashore and took a coach tour around the city. After that, Ted and I walked through the Botanical Gardens and on the "Casbah" where we had to follow a guide (with a tourist party) down through the labyrinth of native Arab quarters - then last of all the Mosque. As the voyage continued, Ted was happy to fill in time playing 'Solo' and Bridge with the same team every day.

I did knitting and crochet while chatting with various passengers or did some reading. There was always plenty of entertainment - deck sports, whist drives, housie, dancing and the cinema. We even had a lot of fun at the Mad Hatters Ball and quite a few concerts impromptu.

The ship's concert was one of the highlights and it was there I first met Patrick O'Hagan, the well known Irish Tenor. He was due for a concert tour of Australia. We also had the pleasure of listening to Madam Fredrika of Austria - she had a beautiful strong soprano voice. The other artists were members of the crew.

Our next stop was Port Said and a group of us went ashore to do some souvenir shopping. Off again through the Suez. Lovely weather until we reached Aden where it was very hot and sticky. We went ashore and I bought two beautifully embroidered blouses and a silk shirt for

Ted. It was very hot through the Indian Ocean to Colombo. We arrived there at 10.30am and sailed at 6.30pm.

It was extremely hot and very few passengers ventured ashore. We stayed on deck all day as the heat in the cabin was intolerable. There was no cool spot anywhere. However, as we left Colombo the weather became cooler. Eight days later we were in Australian waters and berthed at Fremantle for W.A. disembarkation. Ted and I went for a walk to High Street - we only stayed in port for 7 hours. We took three and a half days to reach Adelaide. The sea was very rough with gale force winds and heavy rain. Had to stay a second day at Outer Harbour because the wharfies were on strike. Ted and I went by train to Adelaide, found a good restaurant and then went to a Newsreel.

Two days later - Melbourne. We spent the first day there with Mrs Betty Whitelaw. A personal friend of Ida Maon who we had promised to contact. We had no problem meeting her at Flinders St Station. Ida had sent her a good description which she quickly recognised.

Betty took us to the Australia Hotel for lunch and then a taxi to her home in Hawthorn. We enjoyed our visit immensely. The next day Ted and I made our way to St Kilda but were not very impressed. We had four days in Melbourne, delayed there also by the wharf strike. Finally left December 15th and arrived Sydney on December 17th. The voyage had taken exactly six weeks. We were met by Rita and the children, Daphne, Roger

and Andrew and Bill and Blanche Wigmore.
We were very pleased to get back to Fairfield and Ted
was delighted to find the garden as flourishing as when
he had left it.

The next day Peter and Aileen gave us a lovely welcome
home party. The guests included Aileen's family. The
weather was extremely hot and developed into a heat
wave, 90 degrees all night for nearly a week. Fortunately
a cool change arrived on Christmas Day. We had quite a
gathering. Rita, Frank and family, Peter, Aileen and family, Bill and Blanche Wigmore and everyone enjoyed Santa
and the Christmas Tree.

In the last week of December, both Daphne and Ted
obtained employment with the same firm. Bett's Plastics
at Enfield. during the next few years I looked after
Andrew while his parents and Ted went to work.

We were fortunate to have an excellent young doctor, just
around the corner in the Boulevard - Dr. Ken Cranney.
He attended to all our ailments. He helped Ted
enormously with knee injections for arthritis and all my
many indispositions received successful treatment.
Andrew too was in his care. Dr. Cranney became my
friend as well as my doctor and we have always kept in
touch.

Unfortunately, Daphne and Roger's marriage ended in
1956. They were eventually divorced in 1960. In the
meantime, Daphne met Wal Robbins which culminated in
marriage 1962.

Ted retired in 1958 and this meant a change in lifestyle for us in the future. We discussed plans with the family and our final decision was an application for a War Service Home Loan and build somewhere on the coast.

Wal took us around to look for a suitable site near a beach and we finally found a sandhill at The Entrance North, at the end of the street next to the ocean and a lovely wide beach.

It had taken a few months for the legal and finance procedures to be settled. The next step was to level off the top of the hill ready for building. A bulldozer quickly accomplished this and in due course a builder was contracted and work commenced in May 1960.

1960-1969

Frank and Rita kindly loaned us the Cabin at the rear of their holiday cottage at The Entrance. Ted and I left Fairfield for good on June 6th and we lived in that cabin for six months. Ted went by bus over to our block every day to erect all the fences. Wal and Daphne made frequent trips from Fairfield to the house to do the painting. The plumber was the last of the workmen to leave.

It was suggested that Ted and I go to Sydney to pack up all our goods and chattels still at Stanbrook Street. While we were doing that, Wal and Daphne went north to finish the painting. We were away three days and on December 11th Wal came back, picked us up with all our packages and belongings and we returned to North Entrance. Wal opened the front door for us and we could not believe our eyes. Every room was furnished, completely, with carpet on the floor and a well stocked fridge in the kitchen. In the dining area, a 'party' meal was ready on the table.

Wal's sister Jean and her husband Reg Campbell had helped with all the work. It was incredible. The transformation was such a contrast to the scene we had left three days ago with paint cans and brushes, rolls of wallpaper and dust sheet galore and all kinds of odds and ends scattered everywhere. Now everything was ready for our occupation. Long after the four hard-working team had left that night, we were going from room to room, opening cupboards and finding all kinds of surprises. We named the property "Mungala" an aborigine word meaning 'sandhill'.

The next ten years was a happy period in our lives. Ted loved fishing and I was able to help supply him with bait by catching pipis as they were washed in by the waves and before they disappeared under the sand. When that happened a rapid twist of the heel would expose them. We often walked two or three miles along the beach to a good fishing spot, fished until noon and then enjoyed a picnic lunch before working our way back again.

The prawns were plentiful in Tuggerah Lake and our lantern and prawning nets were in constant use. We only had to cross the sand dunes over the rise from our front gate and we were on the beach. At the far end of our street was Tuggarah Lake. We had ever so many visitors, coming and going all the time. I think they enjoyed the added attraction of our ideal environment. We would all go prawning at night, invariably a good catch from 12lbs to 15bs. If the "run" was not good, there would be sufficient to use for bait.

Ted was a good fisherman and we always had a good supply with enough to share around. Mainly flathead, bream and whiting. Our star fisherman was Andrew. We were always sure of fish when he visited us - he usually fished for whiting. He would fillet them with not a bone being left. On one occasion he won the record for the largest catch of 104 whiting in the shortest time.

Andrew began his training for Naval Officer at Jervis Bay training college in 1967. Wal and Daphne took us to visit Andrew several times in his new quarters.

Mungala *The Entrance North, 1962*

Ted and Queen
45th Wedding Anniversary, 1963

Ted was not very well during the early part of 1968 and had to spend a week in St Luke's Hospital with a heart condition. It was July before he felt well again. I also spent a day in "The Sydney Hospital". The pain I had experienced so strongly was attributed to arthritis. The doctor treating me was Dr. Jeremy, a specialist who had just completed two years in America in arthritis research.

(L to R) Andrew, Daphne and Wal 1968

At that time there was nothing to eradicate the complaint–drugs were only pain-killers. His advice to me was to "stick with Disprin".

We went to Fairfield to spend our Golden Wedding Anniversary with Wal and Daphne.

Wal had added an extension to the house and early that evening they suggested we have a look at it. Ted opened the door to find the new room packed with relatives and friends - forty-six guests. There were tables along two walls loaded with tempting food. It was a beautiful surprise and everyone enjoyed it.

Ted and Hanne Fielder were married in Oslo - Norway just one month later, October 26th, 1968.

During that October, Ted enrolled as a member of the Tuggerah Lakes Memorial R.S.L. Club at Long Jetty, in the special Rehabilitation Centre. He had become good friends with another old Digger, Arthur Young, a widower who lived alone farther down our road.
Ted and Arthur went off together every Monday to learn handcraft at the Club Centre. Ted chose basket weaving and for several years found it very profitable. He made all kinds of baskets and had a ready market for them.

1969

We had the pleasure of a visit for three days with Vince and Al Kernahan, Aileen's parents. They enjoyed the beach.

Soon after we moved to North Entrance in 1960 and had made some new friends, we were asked to join the local Progress Association. This we did and it followed that I became a member of the Ladies Auxiliary.

We had a social afternoon once a month and played "Hoy". The ladies all made cakes and donated all kind of things for sale on the opportunity table to raise funds for the Association. On alternative Thursday evenings, a Euchre party was held in the Progress Hall which Ted enjoyed. Our neighbours, Les and Ailsa Scorgie called and took him in their car. Our social life was quite good and very pleasant. We had frequent trips to Sydney - by Bus to Gosford and then train to Hornsby where either Wal or Daphne would meet us.

We spent Christmas 1969 with Frank and Rita and returned to "Mungala" with Daphne, Wal and Andrew for the New Year and my Birthday.

1970-1979

On 22nd January, Wal came up for us. Daphne had arranged for me to see a skin specialist at St Leonards. The outcome was two rodent ulcers had to be removed from my neck.

We stayed for the Australia Day holiday weekend and during that time it was suggested that we leave "Mungala" and return to the city. We were too far away for immediate help in case of emergency - health or whatever.

We gave the matter great thought. Ted would need to continue with his basket weaving to keep him occupied. I always had plenty of crochet and knitting to interest me. With these thoughts in mind, we agreed to make the change. Daphne and Wal drove us around to look at Units as this was the type of accommodation we had decided would be the most suitable at our age. Wal had noticed a block of units nearing completion in Merrylands, conveniently close to Fairfield and after viewing units at Dundas which did not appeal to us, we set off for Merrylands.

We were agreeably impressed, so much so we would have made our decision and ended the search. However, because this was only the second inspection we had made, it would be advisable to explore elsewhere and see what was available. We covered a wide area surrounding Fairfield but did not find anything which appealed as much as St Ann Street, Merrylands. That was our final choice.

It was close to shops and transport with a large brick garage for Ted to use as his workshop. Situated on the first floor it gave security and with a return balcony we were not shut in. Wal and Daphne took over the whole business of our transfer. They also carried out improvements in the unit itself.

A sideboard and china cabinet to replace a large utility cupboard in the dining area, built in wardrobes and dressing table in the main bedroom and three large floor to ceiling cupboards in the spare room. All very attractive. Everything completed, Wal came up to "Mungala" to collect us and our odds & ends.

We thought we were to go to Fairfield but en-route called at our unit. On arrival we found the place fully furnished, carpet throughout, the fridge and cupboards well stocked, everything ready for our immediate occupation and most the entire family to celebrate with us.

We settled down quickly. Ted met the buyer of the toy Department in Murray Bros Store, Parramatta, by introducing himself and was given a regular order for dolls carry baskets, and junior shopping baskets.

We were able to renew our fellowship with the Christadelphian Ecclesia at Shaftsbury Road, Burwood where we met several old friends. I joined the Dorcas Sisters Class. This class consisted (and still does) of a small number of sisters who meet in our hall on alternate Tuesday mornings to make garments and other necessary items for charity organisations in need of help. Funds were raised for this work by a voluntary collection contributed once a month by the Brethren and Sisters of our own meeting.

The Treasurer of the class bought the necessary materials, buttons, tapes, cotton etc., and a quantity of knitting and crochet wool. I was given the job of making baby matinee jackets, knee rugs or bed covers - all in crochet. Each item as required in turn (in 1985 I made 66 jackets). There were three sewing machines and pyjamas, nightdresses, pillow cases and feeding bibs were completed by the sisters in record time. The large parcels of finished clothing etc. were all donated and sent to a Children's Hospital, the City Mission and the Smith Family. I always brought some crochet work home with me to fill in my spare time. I thoroughly enjoyed doing it and being part of such a worthy cause. The Dorcas Class still exists in our Ecclesias today.

Ted and I enjoyed many little excursions to Parramatta, only ten minutes in the local bus. We shopped mainly at David Jones and always had lunch there before returning home.

Wal called frequently to pick up Ted and take him on the "Wal Robbins" suburban business calls to interview possible clients. Then there were the occasional visits to the Naval College at Jervis Bay to spend a little time with Andrew. We also had regular visits from Frank and Rita. On December 5th 1971, Wal and Daphne gave a big farewell barbecue party for Andrew who was leaving on a world Naval Tour on December 9th.

Wal and Daphne took us to the Airport to see him off. Three days, later while having lunch with Daphne, Wal suffered a fatal heart attack. He collapsed and passed away immediately. The shock to everyone was immense and devastating for Daphne. Contact was made through the Navy to inform Andrew and he decided to cancel his tour and return home.

Time passed and in 1972, Daphne made her first visit to

England. Andrew had left earlier on his postponed Naval transfer and she was able to contact him in Portsmouth. It was here Daphne first met our dear friend Aline. Over the years the friendship became deeper and after she visited Australia we considered her as one of the family and we still do. At the end of 1973, Rita and Frank's third son Bruce married Bev Fawcett on 17th November.

At the beginning of 1974 I had a very heavy cough and cold and Bronchial Pneumonia developed. We called the doctor acting for Dr. Cunningham who was on vacation and she prescribed "Ampicillin". Daphne came over and cared for us until I recovered. Unfortunately this was followed immediately by a severe skin rash. The doctors tried to arrest it but on July 20th I was admitted to Auburn Hospital with a total skin allergy rash. The irritation was almost unbearable.

It lasted for three weeks, after which Daphne took me to Fairfield for another two weeks. Ted was already there. Dr. Cunningham, who attended me, was also Ted's repatriation doctor. During one of their little chats they discovered Dr. Cunningham was the ship Surgeon on board for the last voyage of R.M.S. Chitral to England in which Ted and I were also passengers in 1953. Another unusual co-incidence in my life was that I was able to produce the Passenger List and the Gala Dinner Souvenir Menu Card.

The latter had been autographed by the Surgeon and his signature was still the same and just as difficult to decipher some twenty years later.

Ted & Queen at Bruce & Bev Fielder's Wedding, 1973

The following October Daphne took us, with Jeanie Wearne (a particular friend of ours), for our first visit to Port Macquarie. We spent a very enjoyable five days there exploring everything - its historical buildings and the country-side around it and then we visited friends in Wingham.

The weather was extremely hot and we were very grateful when our air-conditioner was installed as soon as we returned home.

On November 2nd Daphne flew to England. I mention these flights because we missed her so much. She was absent for several months.

1975

New year was very hot as were the following months. Daphne returned from England in April. I was just recovering from a minor stroke which had occurred two weeks previously. I had to stay in bed as my blood pressure was dangerously high and the doctor called every day.

Rita and Frank had flown to England on March 30th so both girls were overseas during my illness. However, Ray and Karen were a great help and came to our aid.

I felt so ill and terribly weak. Our neighbours were wonderful, cooking special meals for us and looking after Ted. I recovered gradually and returned to our normal routine.

In June we received the sad news of the passing of our much loved and close friend in England, Jack Mason.

September 5th Andrew left the Navy.

We had a delightful holiday for twelve days in November.

Daphne took us to the "East Mullane" property, 46 miles from Walgett, not a great distance from the Queensland border. Ted enjoyed being in the bush again and I had never been to the outback. Taking a walk down the paddock from the homestead, we soon saw plenty of birds and wild life in the scrub and between stunted trees groups of kangaroos and emus who quickly disappeared as we approached. We even saw a Bower bird's nest, built on the ground in the centre of a large tall clump of dry grass, supported by twigs and leaves. A wide area of the ground in front of the nest had been carefully cleared of dead leaves and sticks from the trees close by and replaced with small pieces of coloured glass, fragments of crockery and shiny bottle tops. The nest was not far from the house so it was easy to guess where the male bird had found his display to please his mate. It was all neat and tidy.

1976

Late in April, Daphne received news that her great friend Aline, of Portsmouth England was ill in hospital and her family were finding it difficult to cope with all the business affairs. Daphne promptly decided to go over and help them and flew out on May 1st.

In June I came down with a vicious type of influenza and was confined to bed. My cough was terrible and proved hard to get rid of it. The doctor made frequent visits and Rita came up and looked after us. Daphne phoned from England concerning my health - Aline was still in hospital.

Ted did not get the flu but was very restless at night, especially on 24th July when he was really sick. I called the doctor who thought the symptoms indicated flu (the vicious one) was about to develop.

Ted & Queen at East Mullane, 1975
(last photo of Ted)

However, the next day he was much better and enjoyed his meals but that night he was as restless as ever. Got up and walked around. I went back to sleep but was awakened by a loud crash. Ted had got up, did not put the light on and mistook the reflected light in the dressing table opposite the window for the bedroom door. He walked into the furniture, lost his balance and fell heavily to the floor landing on his knees. I could not possibly help him - he was too big and heavy and any attempt I made was too painful for him. I placed a chair with a pillow for him to lean on and phoned for the Radio doctor. I then phoned Andrew at Fairfield and managed to wake him. He was there in no time and so capable. I was able to calm down. By moving Ted's bed across the room to him, Andrew managed to get Ted off his knees and on to the bed before the doctor arrived about 4.30am.

After his examination he told me Ted had broken his hip, said he would get in touch with Dr. Cunningham as soon as possible and would send an ambulance to convey Ted to Concord Hospital. I phoned Ray and he was here before it arrived which was good timing because it took two Ambulance Officers, Andrew and Ray to carry Ted down the stairs on a stretcher. I went in the Ambulance with Ted and Andrew followed behind. On arrival Ted was taken immediately to the X-Ray department and Andrew took me back home. Rita and Frank visited him in the afternoon and Andrew & I returned at 6.00pm. Both of the visits were very brief, Ted was in a lot of pain and had been heavily sedated. Another day passed before the operation was performed, he came through that successfully but no visitors were allowed. Andrew kept Daphne informed and she phoned Australia as well.

Ted remained under light sedation for three days which made him very confused. I was very relieved on July 31st to find him rational again. All the family visited him in turn and he was very pleased to see Aileen and Peter & Peter's sister Barbara. He wanted to see "Dap Dap" (her childhood pet name) and accepted that was not possible because she was still in England caring for Aline.
Andrew, Ray and Helen provided transport for me - also Irene Butcher - a close friend.

After three weeks, Ted was sent to the Lady Davidson Convalescent Home. Flu had been raging in his Ward - he was a victim and still had a very bad cough.
As a result, two days after his transfer he was unable to take physiotherapy and his chest had to be drained, again no visitors.

Sunday 15th August, Jan and Rita took me to the Home. He looked very tired and he had lost weight but was sitting out in a chair. He was quite cheerful and stood up unaided to welcome us.

Before Ted had this recent fall, whenever we went shopping together, whichever store we were in, he would find a seat and say "I'll wait here for you" and I would finish looking around and shopping and return to him and there he was, always with a smile for me.

On this particular day - August 15th - as we were about

to leave, I assured him it would not be long before I could take him home. He took my hand and said "I'll wait here for you until you come". We left at 3.20pm and as I kissed him goodbye he gave me a little hug and said "I love you". Little did I dream those would be his last words to me.

Andrew called to see him shortly after our departure and told us later he had spent quite some time with "Pop" and had discussed the price Andrew had paid for a dog. The following morning, 16th August 1976, Ray and Andrew called to see me. They brought the almost unbelievable sad news that my dear Eddy, as I had always called him, had suffered a fatal heart attack and passed away at 11.30am. It was a terrible shock to me, so hard to realise.

Apparently Ted had been taken to the Physiotherapy Block to commence his exercises for the hip replacement (which would have been quite an ordeal for him) and whilst there, collapsed and did not survive - just two weeks away from his 84th birthday. A good age for a veteran of two World Wars and as time progressed, I realise God had been very merciful in Ted's final discharge.

I had been the Bride of an Anzac 58 years.

Rita stayed with me for three days. Daphne, who had been informed by Andrew of all that had happened, was already on her way home. She arrived at 10.00pm the following night.

The Cremation was at Rookwood Cemetery August 19th and some time, later on, the Ashes were interred beneath a young Bangalay Gum Tree by the side of the lawn in Andrew's garden at the Yarrabar Pottery, Dubbo, the city of Ted's birth and family.

In the book "Dubbo, City on the Plains" by Marion Dormer, Ted is mentioned and described as "a great character". He was jovial, generous and always willing to help anyone. Like all human beings he had his faults, so have I, but you learn to cope with them.

Before the chapter on my Anzac husband is closed, I must say this Anzac Bride was always loved and cared for in spite of many trials. Like all married couples we had our ups and downs, differences of opinion - yes - but we never had an argument. Any of our close friends or members of our own family can verify this statement. We agreed to disagree and changed the subject. This sounds magnanimous. We made that special decision early in our marriage - just a few weeks after I arrived in Australia. To illustrate the origin of our resolution I will relate the incident which created it and it will reveal Ted's easy-going nature.

I cannot recall the subject of our lively discussion. We had only just got up and dressed and had not left the bedroom. There was no bathroom in that primitive old homestead. Personal cleansing took place in the bedroom using a large crockery bowl with a matching water jug, on a wooden washstand.

I have never been a person to sulk but this particular morning I was so disgruntled, I childishly decided I would not answer Ted when he spoke to me. He made two or three attempts to restore my good humour but I refused to reply and he went away. A few minutes later he returned to our quarters carrying an enamel bowl of warm water, a cake of strong disinfectant carbolic soap in his hand and a clean towel tossed over his shoulder. He greeted me with a grin and said "Darling, you forgot to wash your ears this morning, please do it now". How could I misbehave any longer! The trouble he had taken made us both laugh, kiss and make up. It taught me a lesson I never forgot.

In the next few months I had to get used to living alone without my partner, so sadly missed. My friends and family were very helpful with their visits and I gradually settled down. My crochet filled my spare time.

November 6th, Jan and Phillip Clift were married.

Aline arrived from England in November and stayed until March. The friend who accompanied her, Eileen Harley, went home before Aline.

Mid - December I had the pleasure of meeting the Irish Tenor, Patrick O-Hagan again. Our first acquaintance had been on board "Maloja" as fellow passengers in 1953. He had been booked by A.B.C. Television for a special program. Ted and I were returning home after our long holiday.

On this current occasion, it was advertised Patrick
O'Hagan was in Sydney and would give a performance in
the Regency Curt, Westfield Parramatta. With two of my
local friends we attended. After the show ended, I went
to the stage and re-introduced myself and handed him the
"Maloja" souvenir concert program with his own signature
and message written on the back, which I had taken with
me. He was really pleased to see me and without any
further ado, put his arms around me and kissed me
affectionately. A press photographer noticed us and
quickly used his camera. I was given a copy later by the
newspaper office which published it.

On Christmas Day we had a family party at Bruce and
Bev's home.

1977

January 2nd was my 80th Birthday.
Daphne had organised a special celebration party for me.
It was held on board the John Cadman Ferry Restaurant.
It was a beautiful day and we had a sight seeing cruise
right around Sydney's spectacular Harbour.
On our return we all went to Rita and Frank's home to
cut the decorated cake Rita had made. Peter and Aileen
and Aileen's mother, Al Kernahan were among the guests.
We had a lovely evening.

January 18th Hanne offered to bring my dear friend Sister
Ann Gilham, resident at the Christadelphian Home at
Padstow to visit me. They were late arriving here owing
to traffic congestion and delays caused by a railway

*With Patrick O'Hagan, Christmas 1976
at Westfield Parramatta.*

disaster at Granville Station. A concrete overhead bridge had collapsed and fallen on to a passenger train below as it passed under. 83 people died, 213 injured. It was Australia's worst train disaster.

The year progressed. Unfortunately on September 4th, Daphne had a very nasty accident. She cut three toes on her right foot while using the lawn mower. It was Sunday, which made it difficult to find an open surgery. Andrew brought her to the Merrylands Medical Service but the doctor there sent her on to Casualty Department, Parramatta Hospital. Daphne had 9 stitches in her little toe and three stitches in the next one. She had to return to the hospital in four days for dressings.

I went to Fairfield to help. Daphne has always been conscious of the discomfort of losing the greater part of her toe. Incidentally the shoe she had worn was slashed beyond repair.

Crochet still kept me busy. I made large Afghan rugs for each member of the family. Robyn Stewart from Orange asked me to make a rug suitable for her daughter Lynne's bed, I was happy to have the opportunity to do something for our real friends. Bob supplied me with the wool and I finished making it in 35 days. It met with full approval.

On December 31st, Daphne flew to England. 1977 progressed in an uneventful fashion.

1978

I spent a great deal of time at Bulls Hill Pottery while Daphne was overseas. She returned home on May 7th. We then had to get busy choosing and buying our outfits for Andrews wedding. Andrew married Lesley Anne Selwood. The Ceremony took place at St John's Church, Ashfield and the Reception at "Amory" in the same locality - July 28th 1978.

On November 22nd, Frank Fielder announced his retirement and a very happy family party at the St George Leagues Club marked the occasion. Our next family gathering was on Christmas day which was spent at the home of Jan and Phillip.

1979

I went to the pottery frequently with Daphne and was occupied there with weighing and rolling clay to various given weights.

Syd and Nell Percival from Campbelltown came to visit me quite often and of course the old days at Pine Farm were always recalled.

Daphne's long term friend Gwen Hallam invited me on many occasions to morning tea or else in the afternoon, she would call and pick me up in her car and take me to her home "Canary Cottage" at Canley Vale, where she had a fascinating garden.

Aline wrote to me from England later in the year and said she proposed to bring her daughter Lorraine to spend Christmas in Australia. She asked if we could keep it as a surprise for Daphne. Accordingly on 19th December, after much secret planning, Rita and Frank met the visitors at the airport and brought them to me at Merrylands for lunch. We knew Daphne had a friend to lunch with her at Fairfield. I phoned and asked her to call in when taking the friend home.

We did not have long to wait before Daphne rang my door bell. Aline went and opened the door. The complete surprise and the greetings were ecstatic. Daphne was genuinely astonished. Usually it was she who accomplished all the surprises, now it was our turn. The following week we had a lovely Christmas family party in Daphne's garden, the weather was great, not too hot.

1980-1989

1980 was a very special year.

I had been able to attend the Christadelphian Meetings regularly through the kindness of my friends Bro. Jack and Sister Esma Drake. They lived at Parramatta and drove to Merrylands to collect me.

Aline and Lorraine flew back to England in March with a promise from Daphne that she would return the visit later on. With this promise in mind, Daphne often spoke of going overseas and on one occasion strongly offered to take me with her. At first I declined and dismissed the idea. I was 83 years of age and thought such an adventure could cause problems.

I will admit too that I was a little apprehensive about flying, something I had never experienced. I gave it a great deal of thought and finally decided I had nothing to lose. I would be able to see my brother Fred and his family once more and my home town Salisbury in Wiltshire.

My decision met with general approval and Daphne began making plans and bookings straight away. Dr. Cunningham gave me a complete check-up and stated there were no health problems at all.
April 18th was a very important day. Andrew's little daughter "Jessica Rose" was born. I very much appreciated her parents choice of 'Rose' for her second name in order to maintain a family tradition on my mother's side for many generations.

In June I had a very enjoyable day. Daphne took me and Gwen Hallam to the Fruit Bowl at Bilpin, then to the highway Cafe at Lithgow for lunch, after which we went to the old Zig Zag Railway and rode in the steam train to Bell and back.

Daphne and I had many shopping sprees in preparation for our approaching overseas trip. We were booked with Qantas to fly to England on 25th July via Singapore and Bahrain. Five days before our departure, the family gave us a lovely "send-off" party which was held at Ray and

Helen's home. On the 25th July we left for the Airport at
11.00am and were delighted to find so many family
members and friends waiting to wave us off. Lunch at
the 'Jet Restaurant' was almost another party. Our flight
was called at 2.00pm and at 3.00pm exactly we moved
out - a wonderful take off and I knew I would enjoy
everything. Our seats were most comfortable with plenty
of leg room.
We sat in the front row of the business section up a short
spiral stairway, only two seats in a row so we were not
disturbed by other passengers.

We reached Singapore at 10.30pm (Aussie time). The
jumbo was cleared for fumigation and passengers went by
bus to the air terminal shops then returned later.
We were off to Bahrain in a very short time. At 3.30am
we landed and spent the interval in the very hot and
steamy terminal shopping. We were glad to return to the
plane with London the next stop. The flight was
beautiful, so calm and steady. I enjoyed it thoroughly.
Daphne and I played 'rummy' and read our books to pass
the time. When we settled for the night, I slept for five
hours undisturbed.

The next morning I had a good wash and change then
breakfast. Half an hour later the steward took the two of
us into the cockpit and introduced us to the Pilot –
Captain Morris. He was very friendly and as we were
then flying over the city of Baghdad he identified several
points of interest, including the river Euphrates. We were
flying at 25,000 ft, it was a most enjoyable interlude and a
very special privilege.

July 26th we landed at Heathrow, the London Airport.
Jack and Aline were waiting for us and eventually we
were in the car on our way to Southsea. I had slept
another two hours after leaving Baghdad and I think all
the sleep I had on the plane eliminated any jet-lag. I did
not experience that at all.

We reached Southsea at lunch-time, after which I phoned
my brother Fred and his wife and made arrangements to
meet. Our host and hostess Jack and Aline had purchased a four berth caravan in which they intended to
take us on tour. To our amusement when we went to
view this vehicle, it bore the name "Tortoise" (in my
honour) painted in large letters above the rear window.
The caravan was a delight with ample space for the four
of us to be quite comfortable. It was divided in the
centre by a folding screen partition which afforded
privacy when required. Fridge - cupboards - stove - sink
and toilet.

It was great meeting my folks again, they gave us a warm
welcome and we had lots to talk about. Our first caravan
tour was to the West Country down to Lands End in
Cornwall. We set off in good weather for the New Forest
where we camped among the trees and the forest ponies
came to visit us. The next day we passed through
Ringwood, Wimborne, Dorchester, Bridport to North
Seaton and its Shrubbery Farm park. We had a rest and
change then Jack took us into Lyme Regis for dinner.
Where it was possible, we drove around the various
towns to have a look at the old buildings and churches.
For instance, we were able to pull up and visit the

centuries old Minster at Wimborne. The main problem was being able to drive a big car, towing a caravan through the extremely narrow streets of these ancient places - not always possible.

We continued our travels and some two and a half hours later found a good camp site, had lunch and then went for a drive across Dartmoor. The country was very bleak and rocky, huge boulders everywhere. We passed the grim exterior of the notorious Dartmoor Prison on our way to Princetown where we had a genuine devonshire cream tea, then left for Paignton and Torquay. We stopped there for drinks before leaving for Totnes, Plymouth and Tavistock. It was 11.00pm by the time we returned to the caravan at Harford Bridge. Off again in the morning to Tavistock and across to Badmin Moors to Redruth, Camborne and St Ives, Hayle and Pendeen. At Pendeen we found 'Bed & Breakfast' at "the Smugglers Haunt". This ancient village inn was 300 years old with low beamed ceilings, inglenook fireplaces and lattice windows. After a good night and then a generous breakfast we left the van and departed for Land's End. It was raining.

By the time we reached our destination it was a deluge with gale force winds. Jack lent me his waterproof jacket with hood - it was full length on my short figure and kept me quite dry. We disregarded the weather and walked through the little souvenir shops on the sea front. Jack and Aline held me quite firmly, so strong was the wind as we posed for the camera by the international sign post near the edge of the cliff, a very rugged rocky coast line indeed. We doubted the success of the photography under such wet conditions but the snaps were quite good after all.

On our visit to this famous promontory in West Cornwall in the year 1980, the whole area was in its natural state. Today there are tourist barriers and expensive entrance fees for every attraction.

Next day we left "The Haunt" and drove to Penzance. We had a good look around then went to Padstow for a lunch of Cornish Pasties. We continued to Tintagel where we visited "The Pixie Houseî. Bude was our next stop where we found an excellent bed & breakfast. The following morning after a gourmet breakfast, we went for a walk around the town. We explored the "Cornish Stone Company'sî Jewellery Store, where local amethysts of all shapes and sizes were set in all kinds of jewellery. There were also a selection of stones not set. I bought a little single stone dress ring. Andrew had given me some money to buy a souvenir keepsake of our trip and this was my choice. I also bought an amethyst for Rita.

We left Cornwall and proceeded to Clovelly in Devonshire. It was cold and wet so I remained in the store while the others rambled. I had been there before and in better weather. We moved on to Torrington for lunch, then on to Okehampton with its narrow streets for some shopping. We camped at Mary Tavy. The next day Daphne and I decided to stay with the caravan and have a rest while Jack and Aline went on a little excursion of their own. We had a hot chicken dinner in "Tortoise" later in the evening, with a lovely steamed pudding which Aline had made. Our next camp we thought suitable was at Millbrook House but before we could drive in we were interviewed, to our private amusement, by two elderly ladies. They appeared to be exact replicas of characters in Jane Austen's books.

They wore long black dresses, tight bodice and sleeves with very full skirt. (Lace mob caps were missing.) I was wearing an ordinary floral three quarter length summer frock but it did not meet with their approval – just utter disdain and the comment "Much too short". We were the only campers there. One more day travelling back to the New Forest and one more night in the caravan. From there we drove straight home to priory Crescent, Southsea. It was ten days since we left, all the sight-seeing and places visited as well as the picturesque camp sites, together with complete comfort in the caravan, made it an enjoyable, unforgettable experience. The date August 9th, 1980.

Nine days later the four of us set off for London. Jack drove us through the city, right around the walls of Buckingham Palace, Admiralty Arch, Trafalgar Square and Piccadilly before taking us to a flat in the Roman Way, Islington.

The next morning Daphne and I walked to the Caledonian Road Tube Station in the next street and went on the underground railway to Knightsbridge and so to Harrods. It was magnificent - every department had a spectacular display, so much to see and admire. We enjoyed our shopping and exploring and our lunch. On our way back to the station, Daphne bought some shoes and slippers in Rayne's famous shoe store.

During our stay in London, we all went to see "The King and I" staring Yul Brunner at the Palladium Theatre in Argyle Street. The next day we all went to the Adelphi Theatre in the Strand to see "My Fair Lady". Two excellent shows in two grand old buildings.

The next day we packed up and returned to Southsea and prepared for our next trip. We planned to take a caravan tour of the east coast area of France. We had almost finished loading up when we heard the news that the French fishermen were blocking the seaports and no passenger ferries were running across the Channel. Going to Scotland was also on our agenda and as we were all set to travel, we decided to go north to the Highlands the following morning.

During the radio breakfast news it was announced the French Navy had moved in and ended the fishermen's blockade and that all ferries would be running as usual. After several phone calls, Aline was able to book us on a ferry from Portsmouth Docks to Le Havre, France at 3.00pm. Jack and I left immediately with car and caravan, as we knew there would be a long wait in the queue to drive the vehicles on board. The girls finished the last minute jobs and came by train. We sailed just after they joined us right on the dot of 3.00pm. It was a lovely crossing quite smooth all the way. We had dinner in the restaurant on board and arrived Le Havre 9.10pm.

We were soon ashore and travelling towards Garnneville. It was very dark and after about eight miles we decided to camp for the night in a lay-by.

In the morning we were awakened by men shouting very loudly in French. We were not, as we thought, in a lay-by but were parked right across the entrance of a large building supply premises and the men could not drive in to report for work.

It began to rain but we travelled on having our meals in the caravan. Aline did an excellent job with the cooking and we eventually reached Champroset, in the Normandie Forest and stayed the night. It was fine the next morning and we continued through a rural area and Aline obtained some fresh milk from one of the farms. Our next stop was Chateau Gontier, on the river Maine, a charming little village with several small shops. We all went for a walk before retiring.

It was decided to travel as far south as possible the next day and we passed through many small towns with extremely narrow winding streets and ancient buildings. We admired Angiers (quite a big city) on our way to the beautiful Loire Valley. The Loire Valley is wine country. Acres of vineyards were on each side of the road. We stopped in brilliant sunshine at one of the wine booths and were invited by the vendor to taste several different wines. We each bought a bottle of our own choice.

We proceeded to Chantonnay, quite a big town and we

decided to book into one of the hotels for the night, where we could have a hot bath and change before dinner. We left after breakfast the next morning, through St Hermine, a large town, then Lucon and on to La Tranche, again the streets were extremely narrow. We found a camp site not far from the sea. Next day we kept travelling until we reached Fortenay le Conte on the river Vendee, where we stopped for coffee at a pavement cafe, then went on to the Venise Verte district - a miniature Venice.

We hired a boatman to take us along the numerous canals through the lush green country. It was very beautiful through all the trees. The boatman stood at the rear of the boat and propelled us along with a slender pole. It took exactly one hour to complete the circuit. On our way again to Coulon where we saw a lovely old Abbey and had a look through it.

It was great travelling in this fashion. We could stop and explore anything along the way in our own time. We eventually reached Surgeres where we stayed the night in the "Hotel Gambetta". We all went for a walk before retiring. Early breakfast and then a look around the town, including a visit to the Bank. From there we drove straight on to La Rochelle, on the coast.

Jack parked our vehicles and he and Aline went to have a look at the Harbour while Daphne and I went to the shops. Two and a half hours later we all met and went to a camp site at La Griere near the sea where we stayed for three days. Jack and Aline enjoyed the beach.

During this time Daphne and I proposed to leave the
caravan and go to Paris by train. We put the suggestion
to the others and they readily agreed, saying they would
meet us one week later. This would give us more time in
Paris than travelling three days by road. Jack and Aline
could please themselves as to when they would get to
Paris.We all got up at six o'clock the following morning
and had tea and toast. It was still dark as we left La
Griere to get the train to Paris from Les Sables, quite
some distance away. We made it and at 8.46am Daphne
and I were on our way, travelling via Angiers and Le
Mans. The carriage was very high from the platform.
We had to climb three narrow vertical steps to get us in

the door, with no hand-rail to help to mount them. The
journey took six hours and by the time we reached our

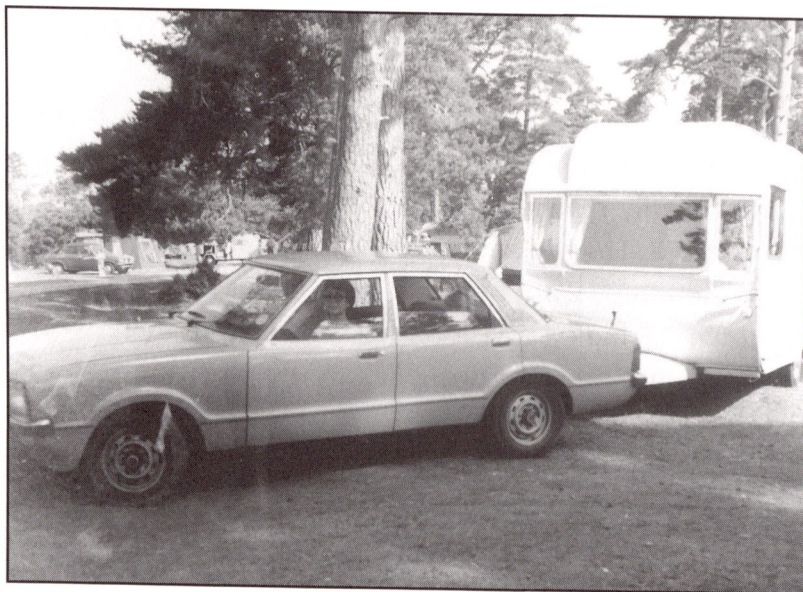

Car and Tortoise, *in France*

destination, we both needed refreshments. There was no dining car on the train.

We took a taxi to the tourist bureau in the Champs Elysses to secure accommodation. We were directed to the Amsterdam Hotel. It turned out to be very third rate with no meals so Daphne set off the next morning to find something better. She was able to book us into the "Hotel Ambassador Concorde" on Boulevard Haussman , a very spacious building. The porter was quite concerned when he could not find any luggage to bring up to our apartment. Daphne explained we had our overnight bags with us and the rest was coming by car later.

We were close to the opera house and Place de la Concorde with its statue of Louis XV. We explored all the attractions and went up in a lift to the first platform of the Eiffel Tower. Of course we visited the shops and I could not resist buying a couple of dresses at a reasonable price.

Another day we went on a "Seineorama Bus Tour" which included a cruise on the River Seine where we went under 22 bridges. I thought this trip was somewhat spoiled by the very strong petrol fumes on board. Les Invalides containing Napoleon's Tomb was very interest-ing. Daphne phoned the Globe Hotel as pre-arranged and made contact with Jack and Aline who came to see us and make final plans. They went off to Moulin Rouge Theatre and we decided to visit Mont Martre again. Our hotel Commissionaire signalled to a passing taxi for us and we seemed to travel at terrific speed. We had our evening meal at a table under one of the huge red umbrellas. We left by taxi at 10.35pm and hurtled back through still crowded streets to our hotel.

After breakfast the next day, we went shopping in a different direction. A taxi took us to Rue du Louvre and we found a lovely shoe shop. I bought a pair of tan shoes in soft plaited leather. That day was 12 September 1980 and now in 1996 I still wear them constantly, having had them re-soled twice.

Aline and Jack joined us that evening and we had a late supper at a pavement cafe. The following morning we said farewell to Paris. The uniformed porter came to our apartment to collect our luggage and escort us down the stairs and through the foyer to a waiting taxi. He carried our two overnight bags and seven large plastic shopping bags with as much dignity as though they were the expensive luggage he was accustomed to. The humour of the situation appealed to us as we were driven away. We went to the Globe Hotel where Jack and Aline were waiting and we all left together for the Railway Station and travelled by train to Versailles. Jack had left the car at the station and the caravan already parked among the trees in a lovely camp site the previous day. We stored our luggage, had a cuppa then Jack drove us to see the famous, enormous Versailles Palace and Gardens. As we were preparing to retire that night we saw a spectacular display of fireworks not too far away and we watched them until nearly midnight.

We set off for our long drive to Le Havre at 10.00am the

next morning and followed the motorway right through.
We stopped at a lay-by (with toilets), had ham and tomatoes for lunch and a cuppa in the caravan, then continued
on our way passing through several toll gates.

At dusk we found a beautiful camp site in the centre of
the Montgeon Forest. After our evening meal, we played
Scrabble until bed-time. We left this lovely spot at 6.45am
and reached Le Havre docks at 7.35pm. We were put
into line ready for loading and finally sailed at 9.00am.
After a fairly smooth crossing, we docked at Portsmouth
at 2.10pm September 15th, 1980.

We were soon ashore and on our way home to Priory
Crescent, Southsea. Two days later Daphne and I went to
Midge & Alec's wedding, Midge is my niece, Fred and
Ad's youngest daughter. It was a very happy occasion
and we were able to meet several other members of our
English family among the guests.

Jack and Aline went to London for a few days and when
they returned Daphne and I did likewise. We went by
train to Waterloo Station and then by taxi to The
Cavendish Hotel on Jermyn and Duke Streets, opposite
Fortnum and Mason. Daphne had booked our accommodation by phone from Southsea. It was the hotel used for
the television program "The Duchess of Duke Street".

We spent six busy days in London and some of the
highlights were attending Evensong in Westminster Abbey
on Sunday night, dinner in Garner's Steak House in
Regent Street and The Tate Gallery. Meals and snacks at

Fortnum and Mason where we also saw the complicated mechanism of their famous clock with its moving figurines in action. Other shops included Simpson's & Swan & Edgars & Marks and Spencer.

On our last day Daphne went to Qantas and booked our return flight to Australia on October 19th. She was fortunate in securing the two front seats in the section upstairs so once again we had plenty of room for our legs and hand luggage.

We had dinner that evening at Wheelers Fish Restaurant in Apple Tree Yard off Duke of York Street. When we returned to our hotel of all cars in London, the Lord Mayor of London's car was parked in Jermyn Street. A big shiny black Rolls Royce. W E I its identification. The next morning we packed, took a taxi to Waterloo Station and were soon back home.

The following afternoon we had tea with Fred & Ad and spent the evening making arrangements to visit Winchester and my childhood home "Sunset View" on the morrow. Aline had kindly offered us the use of her car. We left in good time and Daphne drove us through many villages and familiar spots which had hardly changed at all over the years but still full of treasured memories for me. Unfortunately, when we reached Sunset View, the current owners were not at home. Having got as far as the front door, we went a little farther and had a look around the garden and fruit trees, sampling the Golden Pippin apples discarded on the ground. We had lunch at the village Pub called "The Cricketers Arms". There was another Inn at the other end of Easton and was called "The Bat and Ball". There must have been some keen cricketers around in previous times.

Fred took us into Winchester where we had a good look around and enjoyed afternoon tea at "The Spinning Wheel" opposite the Butter Cross. Before leaving Winchester, we called in to see my cousin, Norman Denham and his wife Nell and eventually reached Southsea at 7.00pm.

The next day Daphne and I had to go to Dr Stewart's surgery to fill in a Qantas Medical Form regarding passengers over the age of 75 years. A long list of questions with the answers recorded by the doctor. She was highly amused at one incredible question, considering the age group it was supposed to cover. The question was: "Are you pregnant??" With a straight face I replied quite seriously "Not at the moment"!! which the doctor immediately wrote down.

On October 1st, Daphne and I set off on our trip to Scotland. Aline had kindly lent us her car. We drove straight through to Oxford where we could not find any bed and breakfast vacancies. At our last enquiry, the lady of the house said she had a friend who might be willing to accommodate us. She phoned her and we were accepted. We had to drive to a nearby village called Kidlington to find Dr. and Mrs. Burbidge.

They lived in an enormous house which had originally been a Rectory. It stood in one and a half acres of ground and it was built in 1445 and the walls were two feet thick. A lovely old building.

We had a good look around before we left for Blenheim Palace, ancestral residence of the Duke of Marlborough. His elder son, Sir Winston Churchill, the great army leader in World War II was born there in 1874. He died in 1965. We paid one pound entrance fee to go inside the walled garden. Actually there was nothing special to see.

We drove a short distance to the village of Blayden and visited the little churchyard where Sir Winston was buried. From Blayden we went to Woodstock (such a pretty place) and on to the Trentham Gardens, landscaped by "Capability" Brown of 18th century fame. Motoring on via Stratford-on-Avon, the birth place of William Shakespeare, through Stoke-on-Trent to our destination for the day, the Post House Hotel, Newcastle-under-Lyme. We had booked by phone. We spent three days in that busy city. Daphne had some pottery business commitments to attend to. We visited the Gladstone Pottery Museum and the Royal Doulton Showrooms where we saw the new Figurine "Elaine" (with fan) which was not yet on sale. We also went to the Spode Gallery and then to the large Wedgewood premises.

We left there for the Lakes District, stopping for lunch at the Bear's Paw Hotel in Warmingham and later had afternoon tea in the Blue Bell restaurant at Milnthorpe. We then proceeded through the Lakes Reservation Area, down narrow lanes between stone walls to Bowness, right on the shores of Lake Windermere. We booked in at the Old England Hotel which overlooked the water. It was raining heavily so we were unable to explore that evening. It was still raining the next morning but we had a good prowl around before motoring on to Gretna via Kendal. We arrived late afternoon and found excellent accommodation for the night at Surrone House. We walked down the street and saw the old house, with its bow window, famous for the elopement marriages in the Victorian era. A notice board stated one hundred thousand marriages had been celebrated in that small room "Gretna Green".

Daphne phoned Mrs. Elliot at Hawick to obtain directions for us to call and visit her. Barbara Elliot (nee McAlister) had given us the address of her husband Alisdair's mother. We travelled on through Grasmere and saw the home of the poet Wordsworth and shortly after, located without difficulty the right house in the right street. We enjoyed our lunch and talked about Australia most of the time. We left at 3.00pm for Glasgow.

It was dark when we got there and we could not find the hotel we wanted. Daphne asked a pedestrian for directions but his Scottish accent was so strong we were none the wiser so we followed the road signs out to the Airport and spent the night in the Excelsior Hotel. After a drive through the city we left for Edinburgh. We had morning tea at Dumbarton then followed the road right around Loch Lomond to the Lomond Hotel at Tarbet for lunch. We took many snaps of the beautiful scenery along the way. We continued on to Stirling and saw the amazing castle perched on the rocks, then into the city where we parked the car in the "Whistle" Shopping Centre and did some shopping. We then resumed our journey and took the M8 direct to Edinburgh.

Our Post Hotel was easy to locate, being next to the entrance to the Zoo.

We spent three wonderful days in that busy city. We enjoyed an extensive coach tour which took us to Edinburgh Castle. The coach parked on the huge parade level where the annual Military Tattoo is held. We walked across the Drawbridge into the Castle precincts. After that visit we went to Holyrood Palace which was most interesting, so full of the history of Mary Queen of Scots and Lord Darnley.

From there we were taken to St. Giles Cathedral, the Mother Church of the Presbyterian Faith and famous for its beautiful stained glass windows.

We left Edinburgh and proceeded to York, our next stopover. It was Saturday October 11th, a lovely morning and we reached Jedburgh at noon, travelling through glorious scenery. We stopped at the Jedburgh Woollen Mills and did some shopping. Daphne bought a lovely tartan mohair rug for me. We had lunch before driving on to Sunderland. This is a large city, very bright and clean with an attractive sea-front and beach. We arrived at our hotel in York in time for dinner, watched TV and went to bed. Sunday morning was showery. After breakfast we went for a walk to the ancient York Minster. A Church service was in progress so we could only view it from outside. We left York at 10.20am took the A1 Motorway, via Coventry right through to the turn-off at

Swindon for Salisbury - my home town - where we reached the White Hart Hotel at 6.30pm.

I feel I must mention here that when I first went to Salisbury way back in 1913, I greatly admired the structure of this Hotel and envied the guests who entered it through the big revolving glass door into the spacious foyer. The lovely Georgian facade, pillared portico and effigy of hart makes the hotel an impressive landmark in Salisbury.

White Hart Hotel Salisbury

There are 73 bedrooms, three bars, several conference rooms and a massive dining room with chandelier with open parking space for 80 cars at the rear of the courtyard.

It seemed incredible that after 67 years had passed my wish came true. I actually entered through that same revolving door, a guest at The White Hart Hotel. There must be some truth in the old saying "Everything comes to those who wait".

After a comfortable night and a good breakfast, we went for a walk through the old city streets and bought some gifts at the "House of John A'Port", a black and white timbered establishment built in 1475. We eventually returned to the hotel and departed. We drove to Salisbury Railway Station and I was able to show Daphne where my office was situated (still there) and pointed out my bedroom window in the staff quarters visible from the parking area in the railway yard. We set off for Sandown, some 30 miles south on the Hampshire coast, to call and see our old friends Sister Mary and Bro. Alf Roberts. We had a lovely afternoon tea with them and then left for Southsea and Priory Crescent via the New Forest, arriving there at 6.30pm, October 13th.

During the next couple of days Daphne packed our excess luggage into large cartons and posted them back to Australia. On the 16th, Aline drove us to Fareham to see Steve and Chris Barnes and baby Douglas. Steve is an old Navy mate of Andrew's and we have never lost contact.

Friday October 17th Fred and Ad gave us a family farewell party. Very pleasant but hard to say goodbye. We left Priory Crescent the next day. Aline drove us to Heathrow Airport and Jack, who had previously gone to London, met us there as arranged. Daphne booked us into the Heathrow Hotel and Jack and Aline went to their flat. Daphne and I had a stroll around the shops and she bought me a key-ring with a small enamel tortoise tag which I am still using every day. We had to be up early the following morning because the hotel bus left at 9.00am for the Terminal.

Jack and Aline met us at the bus stop where we said our good-byes. My wheel-chair was waiting for the long walk which took us right on to the plane. We walked up the short spiral stairs to the "Hump" and we had the two front seats again with plenty of leg room. We had to wait one and a half hours before the air corridor was clear for us.
We went direct to Bombay, re-fuelled then straight to Perth. We had time to disembark for a while and Daphne phoned Jean and Reg Campbell. Jean is Daphne's sister-in-law and although they live in Perth, Reg and Jean have always kept in touch and visited several times in their car and caravan.

A brief stop at Melbourne and then it seemed a short flight to Kingsford-Smith Airport, Sydney.
Rita, Frank, Ray, Andrew, Lesley and Jessica were there to meet us. We all went to Rita's home for a cuppa then Ray and Daphne took me home to Merrylands. It had been cleaned and prepared for my return by our good

friend of many years Irene Butcher - she was Rene to all of us. She did a marvellous job for both of us each week. It is always good to be home again and so ended a wonderful three months overseas holiday. I have so many happy memories of it - thanks to Daphne and Aline.

It was Gwennie Hallam who gave me the "finale" to our trip. She kindly invited Maria Geyer, Jean Wearne and Pat Bliss for morning tea and lunch at her home in Canley Vale as a little welcome home get-together with our very special old friends. We all appreciated it very much. Pat Bliss and her husband John were our friendly family neighbours for many years with their two children John and Geraldine.

Over the years I had been given the name of "TORT" by our family friend Jack Mason and with whom I frequently corresponded. I may have been a little bit slow on the uptake sometimes but I eventually arrived at the correct topical conclusion.

Andrew spent all his school holidays with us at The Entrance and during a vacation early in the New Year of 1964 he bought me a ceramic tortoise money box and so began my huge collection of tortoises. Friends and relatives have sent them to me from all over the world. All shapes and sizes made from various materials such as pewter, silver, china, ivory, jade and glass to name a few, with many carved from native rock and wood. I have almost five hundred fascinating tortoises. It is marvellous to know, with actual proof, that so many caring people when travelling overseas or local holidays have seen a tortoise novelty, thought of me so many miles away and then bought it for me.

While Andrew was in the Navy, whenever he and one of his fellow officers, Steve Barnes, were in a foreign port, they would always find a tortoise for me. Ray, Helen and Ben have always done the same on their vacations home and abroad. They have found some very unusual specimens. Rita and Frank, Jan and Phil, Ted and Hanne and our good friends Martin and Rita Vella and Daphne have also contributed largely to the collection from their extensive travels.

In early 1981 Daphne had some business commitments in Adelaide and Melbourne. She decided to drive there via the outback and suggested taking three passengers - Mrs. Kent (my friend and neighbour in the units), myself and her cousin Ivy Hopkins from Dubbo. (We had to pass through that city on our way). The three of us were delighted and subscribed equally to cover all expenses. Ivy joined us at Dubbo and we continued to Warren, Nyngan and on to Cobar which we reached at dusk. We had our evening meal at the R.S.L. Club with very genial club members, then stayed the night in an hotel close by. It was a very long trek (the next day) to Wilcannia, with scrub country all the way.

We disturbed a number of kangaroos and emus as we passed on our way to Broken Hill. It was extremely hot. We stayed the night in Broken Hill. Next morning we walked to the extensive Pro Hart Gallery and saw the marvellous collection of paintings. We left the "Silver City" and began another long drive to Gawler, S.A. On arrival there we turned off the main road and went into the Barossa Valley as far as Tanunda, where we decided to stay. Early next morning we explored the huge buildings on the vineyards of that locality, having a small taste of wine here and there as we walked around the premises. We left there for Adelaide where Daphne booked us into the Gateway Hotel.

From our windows we could see the beautiful Cathedral and the Adelaide Cricket Ground. During our three days visit we went shopping and sight-seeing and Daphne completed her business transaction. From Adelaide we travelled along the coast road to Melbourne via Mt Gambier and saw its famous Blue Lake. At Port Campbell, Victoria we had a good view of the huge rock formations called the "Twelve Apostles" jutting into the ocean. On through Geelong to the Hilton hotel, Melbourne. Two days later we travelled to Yass and the following day we reached Sydney and home.

By this time I was well into my 85th year. My hearing had diminished considerably and it became necessary for me to wear a hearing aid.

On the 24th February 1982, Andrew and Lesley's son "Luke Andrew" was born. 1983 was the year of the fire at Bull's Hill Pottery. March 1984 Andrew and his family left Bull's Hill and moved to Dubbo (back to the Sunderland ancestry country!).

Andrew bought a small property, a section of the Bushey Park estate along the Peak Hill Road, now called the Newell Highway. Andrew named the new home "Yarrabar" to coincide with the name of the Yarrabar Creek which runs through the land and built a small log cabin type house and started a pottery.

January 2nd 1987 was my 90th birthday. Daphne, with some help from the family, organised a surprise party for me. It was held at Oatlands House, Parramatta. All the old friends were there, Nora Ford and Syd Percival from the 1929 era on the farm, several Christadelphian members from 1938 and Dr. Ken and Mrs Cranney from 1956. Ted Fielder did an excellent job in providing transport for the elderly church members from the Padstow Rest Home. The list of guests is too long to record in detail. I have mentioned the names of the longest standing ones as an indication of the time and effort Daphne made to locate them as well as all the more recent friends. No wonder it was such a happy success.

During the following year (1988) Andrew and Lesley parted. Fay Baun and her three children Robert, Ingrid and Christopher joined Andrew at Yarrabar.

1990-

By the year 1991, I was having big trouble with my eye sight. Daphne took me to the Eye Specialist in Fairfield who had been my optician for many years. I already knew both my eyes were affected by cataracts. Upon examination the Doctor advised surgery for the right eye.

It meant going into hospital for three days. He suggested I think it over and make my own decision. I was 94 years of age which was possibly in his mind.

In the meantime Daphne had to go to Dubbo. We have some very special close friends living in Orange; Bob and Robyn Stewart. On our various trips to the Central West we always called in to see them and perhaps stay the night. As usual, on this particular trip, Daphne broke her journey to visit them. Robyn's sister Pat, a nursing Sister, called in during the afternoon and in the course of conversation mentioned she would have a very busy time with several cataract operations the following day at the Mid-State Orange Eye Centre.

Thinking about my case, Daphne asked Pat for details of the procedure and was informed the actual operation only took about twenty minutes and only one stitch (five stitches had been the Sydney quote). Next a large pad was secured over the eye and the patient was taken to the recovery room for one hour with tea and sandwiches provided. (no intake of food before surgery). When the recovery period was over the patient was discharged and went home. A return to the centre the next morning to have the pad removed and the eye checked.

Robyn kindly suggested that I come to Orange and stay with them. She would make the appointment at the Eye Centre for me and the whole business would be much better than going into hospital in Sydney (to which I was very much averse). I was only too happy to accept Robyn's splendid offer.

The Eye Centre duly notified me to attend for surgery on March 5th at 1.20pm. Everything happened as Pat had previously described to us.

I was completely conscious all the time and felt no pain or discomfort whatsoever. Dr. Liu, the surgeon, was marvellous and dispelled all my butterflies. I was back in Robyn's home at 4.00pm, with a large pad over my eye. This was removed the following morning at the Centre and my new sight was incredible.

I have recorded this experience because a number of people wondered why I went to Orange for treatment instead of having it done in Sydney. I must admit the fact of no stay in hospital was a big factor in my decision. Later in the year, Friday August 16th, 1991, I had the misfortune to fall and fracture my right leg. I managed to reach the phone and call Daphne. She was here in minutes and promptly rang my doctor who came and phoned for an ambulance to take me to Westmead Hospital. The next morning in the operating theatre, two screws were inserted. I spent nine days in hospital and walked with a frame for a few weeks before progressing to a walking stick until mobile.

1992

My 95th birthday was another big super party, celebrated at Ambrosios Restaurant at Canley Vale. It was a delight to see and be with all the family and so many old friends again. It was a very happy occasion.

August saw the family celebrating again. This time for Martin - my eldest great grandson's 21st Birthday, held in a restaurant decorated for the occasion under the guidance of Hanne. This was the last time I was able to dance.

Christmas this year was enjoyed at Bruce and Bevís home. It was lovely to have all my "Fielder" great grandchildren together at one time - quite rare with Lisa residing in Canada.

August, 1992 Martin Fielder's 21st Birthday.
(L to R back row) Nicole, Bev, Bruce, Hanne, Frank,
Martin, Ted (all Fielders)
Jan & Phil Clift, Helen & Ray Fielder
(centre) Wayne Clift, Katrina & Rita Fielder, Queen,
Daphne, Ben Fielder.
(front) David and Scott Fielder

My very last dance taken with Andrew at Martin's 21st.

Christmas Day 1992 in Bruce's garden.
(L to R back) Scott, Nicole, Katrina, Ben, Aimee, David
(front) Martin, Lisa & Hayden, Queen, Nerida & Wayne.

I had several trips to Yarrabar (Dubbo) with stop-overs at
Orange 1993-94. Bob threatens continually to increase
accommodation charges but no-one takes him seriously!
Yarrabar has an extra appeal for me, it holds a very
special spot in the lawn nearest the house. The ashes of
Eddy, my Anzac husband, were buried beneath a young
Bangalay Gum Tree when it was first planted in memory
of him. Fay and Andrew have a beautiful garden.

The house has been extended and is now spacious and a
really comfortable home. My bedroom - known as "Nan's

Room" is always ready whenever Daphne and I pay a visit during the year and especially for Christmas and my birthday.

Ted's tree Yarrabar

1995

Four years after my first cataract was removed the other eye was impairing my vision. Something had to be done about it. Robyn Stewart came to the rescue again and made my appointment for surgery at the Eye Centre on April 4th. The same procedure as before, no pain and this time no stitches! I was 98 years of age and Dr Liu (the surgeon) explained my new vision would not be as strong as the right eye owing to the damage caused by the cataract and deterioration due to my age. However there was a big improvement for a while. Now as time moves on, my sight is not too good.

1996

I have reached my 100th year. Daphne and I spent Christmas as usual, at Yarrabar and stayed for New Year. The next day was my birthday. Andrew and Fay gave me a lovely 99th birthday party. Rob and Robyn Stewart from Orange, Bill and Suzie with Casey and Joshua from Oak Flats, our Dubbo friends, Meri and Laurie Pryde, Meri's mother, Mrs Joan Packard made up the special guest list. Joan is good company for me and I always look forward to seeing her.

If all goes well and God willing an exciting birthday celebration will be held on January 2nd, 1997 with our friends Aline and Bob Hember from England, Lisa and Ed, my great grand-daughter and her husband from Canada, interstate visitors and of course our own large family and all the circle of local friends.

What more can I say, except that I am so grateful to Daphne for all her loving care and attention. A daughter who always does so much more than just the call of duty. Thanks Daphie.

My 99th Birthday Party at Yarrabar
(L to R back) Robert, Suzie Wigmore, Fay, Andrew, Robyn Stewart, Luke, Bob Stewart, Bill Wigmore.
(Centre) Ingrid, Daphne, Queen, Jessica,
(Front) Christopher, Casey and Joshua Wigmore.

Rita and Frank have been a great help over the years in many practical ways. Rita has kept me well supplied with literature. I still get frequent visits and daily phone calls from them.

Andrew and Fay keep in constant touch, they are always interested in my activities and my general health. After all - Andrew was in my care for several years of his early life which created a special affinity between us. The floral tributes I receive from him and Fay whenever memorable dates occur reveal continuous regard. I always enjoy staying with them at Yarrabar. I get thoroughly spoiled every time.
The great-grandchildren too, make me so welcome it gives me great pleasure to be with them. I must mention Ray, Helen, Aimee and Ben.

Ray is always prompt in solving any problem or difficulty that I encounter in the unit. With Helen and Ben he never fails to come and see me on Anzac Day and they always bring me the traditional Rosemary for remembrance. I really appreciate it.

Anzac Day, 25th April, 1996
with Ray, Helen and Ben

Ray, Helen and Aimee have been a tremendous help with
this book. I thank them.
Special thanks also to Bob and Robyn Stewart, they are
always ready to help in any possible way.
Also Billy and Suzie Wigmore never forget me. I thank all
of my friends, too numerous to mention for all the kind-
ness and consideration for such a long time,
including the Christadelphian brethren and sisters who
come and visit me.
It is only by the grace of God I have reached the century. I
thank Him for all my blessings every day of my life.
In conclusion I will quote the words on a hard card given
to me by Andrew

"Be patient
God hasn't finished with me yet."

Queenie Sunderland

EPILOGUE

1997

To celebrate my 100th birthday a luncheon party was held at "Oatlands House", Parramatta.

There were 92 guests which included Aline and Bob from England, my great grandaughter Lisa and her husband Ed from Canada, Jean Campbell from Perth, Jeanette Wace - Queensland, Andrew, Fay and the Yarrabar clan, Joan Meri and Laurie Pryde, Betty and Phillip Hopkins - all from Dubbo. The entire Stewart family from Orange. Grant and Jo were on holiday in South Africa but returned two days early to attend my party. Dr Ken Cranney - Terrigal, Syd Percival - Campbelltown, John Egan - Maitland.

My grandson Ray Fielder had organised the printing of this book "Bride of an Anzac" and a copy was given to each guest.

On the first Sunday after my birthday, Brother Harry and Sister Clara Pearce arranged a lovely luncheon party held in the Christadelphian Church Hall at Burwood. There were forty members and we all had a happy time together.

My sight had been failing for some time and I could no longer see to read small print. I have always been a great reader and I found it very difficult to accept. I have read the Bible right through many times so now instead of daily reading I sit quietly and recall a lot from memory.

Daphne drove me to "Yarrabar" (Dubbo) to spend Christmas and New Year with Andrew, Fay and family. During the week between Christmas and the New Year, Cynthia Foley (reporter for the *Dubbo Liberal* newspaper) came out to interview me.

1998

Consequently when the *Liberal* was published on January 2nd (my 101st Birthday), my photograph and a charming personal report occupied the front page. The phone did not stop ringing. Win Television noted we were having Open House and asked to come out and interview me. I felt very comfortable and even recited a poem at their request. To our delight it was showing on the local television that evening.

In September, Daphne and I received an invitation to attend Grandparents Day at Dubbo Christian School where Luke was a pupil. I was pleasantly surprised when Luke Robbins was called to come to the stage. He received a silver medal for school community activities. I had a special mention for my attendance from Sydney and once again the TV Channel was busy filming for screening that night.

Dr Richard Read, (Government Historian of World Wars I and II for the War Memorial in Canberra) was visiting Dubbo for an Historical Conference while we were there.

Dr Read's hostess had a copy of my book which he had read. He wished to meet me and requested a short interview.

He was so interested in the Anzacs and World War I stories that I could remember, it was a much longer interview than anticipated. Dr Read accepted a copy of my book to take back to Canberra.

Unfortunately there was a very contagious chest infection virus raging in Dubbo and I became a victim. Two days later, Andrew called the ambulance and I was taken to the Dubbo Hospital. The medical care was excellent and ten days later Daphne brought me home to Merrylands where I stayed for a few days. I was not at all well and Daphne took me to her home in Fairfield. I collapsed on Sunday October 11 during the night and Daphne phoned for an ambulance. I was admitted to Fairfield Hospital.

I had pneumonia and was critically ill. Daphne stayed in the hospital with me the whole time. I am sure her strength helped me. The crisis passed and I recuperated at Daphne's home for four weeks.

During this time we received a request for an interview from Peter Rubenstein, a freelance radio journalist who had been in touch with Dr Richard Read. It was a long interview but all the subsequent events and publicity which followed proved worthwhile.

Because of my recent illness we did not go to Dubbo for

Christmas and my birthday as usual. Andrew, Fay and the family spent Christmas Day with Daphne and myself at Fairfield.

1999

My 102nd birthday celebration was "Open House" at Daphne's home. Rita and Frank and the Fielder family were well represented. I also enjoyed the company of a large number of friends together with the Yarrabar clan and Billy and Suzie Wigmore.

In March we received the goods news from Canada that Lisa and Ed were the proud parents of a baby son - Tyler James. My first great great grandson.

I spent Easter at Fairfield. Ray and Daphne had arranged for my unit to be re-decorated during my absence. It was certainly a joy to come home to everything so fresh and bright.

In November, Janet Hawley of *The Sydney Morning Herald Good Weekend* magazine requested an interview to discuss my life story. The cameramen came too and the end result was a lengthy report with photographs.

Dubbo held its Sesquicentenary Celebrations at the end of November and the committee invited me to cut the birthday cake. Daphne took me to Dubbo for the occasion. The cake measured 1.8m x 1.5 m and weighed 125kg. Six men carried the cake up to the grandstand platform. It was so big, we used Andrew's naval sword to cut it. Again, this event was broadcast in the local newspaper and television.

On December 19th I had a talk with Tim Shaw, live on 2GB.

The next day Channel 9 phoned to ask if they could come and interview me for their "A Current Affair" program. The producer, presenter and two cameramen all arrived the following day.

2000

January 2, 2000 - my 103rd birthday (and third century!) was celebrated at Daphne's along with sixty one family and friends. The Channel 9 cameramen were also there to film my cutting of the birthday cake.   My story was presented on "A Current Affair" on 5th January, nationwide.

Since then, we have been inundated with requests from around Australia for copies of my book. I wrote "Bride of an Anzac" after repeated requests from my family. I never dreamt it would circulate so widely and prove entertaining to so many people.

God has blessed me with the gifts of memory and mentality which I am happy to share and maybe he still has some work to me to do.

Time will tell...

Queenie Sunderland

Three Centuries

It all happened a long time ago
1897 was the year
The Nineteenth Century was on the way out
When Queenie chose to appear

The Twentieth Century soon followed
A whole life span for me
In the early days I started school
Aty the tender age of three

My first ride in a car was in 1912
A Daimler limousine
The running boards were wide and high
And the chauffeur was dressed in green

He wore a peak cap with goggles
Leather gloves nearly two feet long
Highly polished gaiters and boots
One felt he could never go wrong

In 1914 war was declared
With all its anxious strain
Allied troops from around the world
Soon camped on Salisbury Plain

The Anzacs came in 1916
Gallipoli heros all
I was destined to meet a special one
He was big and handsome and tall

I'll admit he was a charmer
He swept me off my feet
Ten months later we married
My trust in him was complete

He brought to Aussie in 1919
To Dubbo of all places
For twenty years I lived on *Pine Farm*
And never kicked over the traces

I've seen many great inventions
Aeroplanes and cars
Telephone, radio, television
But as yet I have not been to Mars

Now the Twenty First Century is here
The computer age it is plain
Nasty things computers
They steal away man's brain

The world is in need of our Lord's return
To end destruction and pain
May each of us live to that glorious day
When Jesus begins to reign.

Queenie Sunderland January 2000